The Complete Guide to

Business
and
Strategic
Planning

for Voluntary Organisations

THIRD EDITION

Alan Lawrie

DIRECTORY OF SOCIAL CHANGE

Published by
Directory of Social Change
24 Stephenson Way
London NW1 2DP
Tel. 08450 77 77 07; Fax 020 7391 4804
E-mail publications@dsc.org.uk
www.dsc.org.uk
from whom further copies and a full books catalogue are available.

Directory of Social Change is a Registered Charity no. 800517

First published 2007

ISBN 978 1 903991 70 1

British Library Cataloguing in Publication Data

A catalogue record for this book is available from the British Library

Cover and text designed by Stephen Strong
Printed and bound by Page Bros., Norwich

All Directory of Social Change departments in London:
08450 77 77 07

Directory of Social Change Northern Office:
Research 0151 708 0136

Contents

Introduction

Developing a strategy or a business plan for a voluntary organisation should be a creative and dynamic process. It should be an opportunity to stand back, review progress and generate a new sense of purpose and direction. It should ensure that the organisation is strong, clear about its prioirities and able to make a convincing case for support. However, all too often planning is seen as a chore that takes people away from providing a service. The plan that is produced is a collection of targets, budgets and intentions that have little grounding in reality.

This book's starting point is that strategic planning is an essential and useful process for any organisation. It is about much more than producing a neat and tidy document. This edition focuses on the process of putting the plan together and on turning the ideas and strategies in the plan into action. Generating paper plans is easy compared with the hard work of managing change and making plans work in action.

What this book is about

1 It aims to help voluntary organisations make clear decisions about their future direction and priorities.

2 It introduces some tools for strategic planning and management.

3 It explains how to draw up and use a business plan.

Why think about business plans?

There are several good reasons to think about business plans.

1 The tougher funding climate and the growth of a 'contract culture' have led some funders to require the production of a 'business plan' before they consider a funding application.

Business plans have their roots in the private sector and are an essential requirement in persuading lenders to back an enterprise. In recent years, like many other management concepts, they have crossed from the profit-making sector to the not-for-profit sector.

2 A recognition by many voluntary organisations that the constant rate of change and consequent uncertainty means that the organisation cannot stand still.

Many managers and increasingly some trustees are expressing the need to clarify the aims of their organisation, to decide what is and is not a priority given the limited resources that exist and to set out a direction for the organisation's future. This kind of management is different from dealing with the day-to-day demands of making sure that the organisation continues to operate. Strategic management is hard. It requires clear thinking, clarity of purpose and the capacity to win others' commitment to the process and convince them that it is not some academic or 'pie in the sky' exercise.

3 The arrival at a point where decisions have to be made about the organisation's future.

A director of one charity described her role as like 'riding a roller coaster that never arrives anywhere, but only gets faster'. Changes in legislation, new funding, short-term priorities and new ways of working mean that organisations often just react to external events and become pulled into activities that either do not fit with the rest of the organisation or are a departure from their original aims. Those charged with the management and direction of the organisation need to take a grip on what they are doing. They need to decide where they are going, not simply respond to external events.

All organisations are going somewhere. The future direction could be about the organisation getting bigger or smaller, working in a particular way or doing more or less of a particular activity. The main theme behind this book is that the people who are charged with managing a voluntary organisation need to ensure that they set the direction and agree strategies for where they want to go.

"If you don't know where you are going you are sure to end up somewhere else."

Mark Twain

Developing a plan for a voluntary or not-for-profit agency is different from producing a plan for a commercial agency. In the voluntary sector measures of success are more complicated than making a profit. Often voluntary agencies have to meet the needs of different interest groups – users, funders, volunteers, supporters – all of whom might have different and even competing expectations.

Strategy in the voluntary sector

The following issues often need to be tackled during strategic planning in the sector.

Not being funder led

Often, despite their best intentions, voluntary organisations bid for and take on projects and activities because funding is available rather than because it meets their goals or needs. A trustee of one agency described how 'we've jumped on whatever funding bus happens to be passing – over the past few years we have been about detached youth work, counselling, drugs misuse prevention, social inclusion and now crime reduction. We have cut our cloth to fit whatever funders are into. As a result we have lost what we are about!'

Being more than a collection of projects

Over the past few years many organisations have experienced a shift from being core funded to bidding for specific projects. Usually the projects are fixed term, have their own identity within the organisation and sometimes little relationship to the other projects or activities in the organisation. As organisations move towards being project based it is important that the host organisation has a clear direction and strategy that connects all the projects together.

Gaining a longer-term vision

Increasingly visions are short term. Policy agendas change fast, new structures, programmes and funding streams are launched and funding programmes rarely last beyond a few years. Such turbulent change makes any long-term planning difficult as organisations jump from one issue to another. Short-term survival becomes the order of the day. In such an environment retaining a sense of a longer-term vision and values is key to ensuring that the organisation keeps its integrity and purpose and does not just jump onto the passing bandwagon.

Being able to say 'no' to ideas, opportunities and demands

Often trustees and workers can feel guilty about saying 'no' to opportunities and ideas that could take the organisation to a new place. However, new ideas do need to be rationally and objectively considered. Do they really meet a need? Have we the capacity to do it? Are the risks manageable? A clear strategy can help an organisation to evaluate new ideas and avoid being sidetracked.

Organisational sustainability

Good strategic thinking and planning can help to build a longer-term future. It is important that strategic thinking goes beyond the short-term perspective of some policy makers and funders and asks questions such as what will happen after a fixed term project ends? and how will the organisation create lasting change rather than temporary solutions?

Being all things to all people

In any organisation there is a danger of trying to cover too many areas and spreading the organisation too thin. Strategic planning is an opportunity to clarify purpose, agree priorities and review activities. This can stop drifting or failing to deliver by trying to do too many things at once.

> 'My organisation is brilliant at making priorities. We've got hundreds! Each time we have a planning meeting we get more!'
>
> Director of a local voluntary organisation

Not simply doing something because you have always done it

Tradition and history play a part in any organisation. Precedents are set. Budgets and work plans are drawn up on the basis of the past year's performance. Once something is in imbedded in an organisation's structures and routines it can become a permanent fixture. It is useful to occasionally spend time reviewing why we do things and challenge if they are the best way of using limited resources and energy.

The culture resists change

A voluntary organisation can be a complex place. Often its workers have a relationship to it that is different from other workplaces: a personal or emotional relationship and commitment to the organisation's cause. This can be very positive, but sometimes makes change difficult. Often there are contradictions. A worker in a campaigning organisation describes this: 'we have a very radical mission – as an organisation we are all about changing the world – but internally, it's different simple changes like reducing the number of meetings are met with incredible resistance!'

Funders and business plans

Increasingly, funders, commissioners and purchasers ask or expect to see a business plan as part of the bidding process. Contact with a range of funders identified six main issues that they expected to see addressed in the business plan:

1 To understand the idea behind the organisation or bid.

The plan should set out the 'big idea' behind the organisation. What is the vision that holds the organisation together? How is it different from others? It needs to set out a compelling picture of what the organisation is aiming to do and also what it stands for.

2 To ensure that the plan has been fully worked out.

Increasingly funders need convincing that an organisation's strategy and intentions have been thoroughly and objectively worked out. A secretary of a charitable foundation described how 'increasingly, our funding panel want to know that an organisation has properly thought through what it wants to do rather than being led by its interest or passion'.

3 To check that the organisation is being realistic.

The plan needs to balance being ambitious and realistic. All commitments and targets must be backed up with costings and measurable plans.

4 To ensure that the organisation has thought about possible risk.

Every plan involves some sort of risk. A business plan needs to show that the main potential risks have been identified, analysed and that action has been taken to prevent them. The plan should show that the organisation has systems, processes and contingencies to prevent and monitor risks and enable it to act should they occur.

(continued)

> ## Funders and business plans (continued)
>
> **5 To check that the organisation has the capacity to deliver.**
>
> A programme manager for a government initiative commented that: 'plenty of organisations have brilliant ideas that are relevant and worthwhile, but the plan needs to convince us that the organisation has the management ability and experience to turn an idea into something that delivers'. The plan needs to show that the organisation has the systems, people and structures to manage properly.
>
> **6 To understand the longer-term picture.**
>
> The plan needs to show that the organisation is not just going from one event or funding opportunity to another. The plan should show that as well as having short-term plans that the organisation has a longer-term vision.

Why do a business plan?

There are many reasons to put off or avoid doing a business plan or think strategically:

- Just continuing to operate on a day-to-day basis is enough of a struggle.
- The language of organisational planning can be off putting.
- The word 'business' is objectionable to some people.
- It is difficult to plan in a period of constant change.
- The fear of finding that the 'goal posts keep moving'.
- The lack of skills or resources to implement the plan.

The following six points explain the thinking behind this book and might suggest reasons why voluntary agencies should spend valuable time on the process of creating a business plan.

A paradox about planning

There is a paradox about planning. The harder it is to plan the more important clear planning becomes. Uncertainty about funding, lack of clear direction, a reliance on what was done in the past as the basis for deciding what to do next and a vision that stops at the end of the current financial year means that an organisation can easily become motionless. It spends its time hoping that things will get better. In effect, it becomes governed by what it did in the past rather than what it wants to do in the future. It becomes predictable and paralysed in a rapidly changing world. At some stage someone needs to be bold enough to suggest a direction to go in and to agree a plan for achieving it.

Direction planning rather than a detailed blueprint

In the 1960s and 1970s large corporations and public agencies invested heavily in corporate planning. These planners produced comprehensive ten-year documents that even in more stable times became quickly out of date or even were out of date the day that they left the printers. Our capacity to predict the future accurately is very limited. This book is concerned with helping organisations clarify their long and short-term goals, explore future possibilities and make a case for why others should have confidence in their organisation. It is the process that is important rather than the product.

The process and the results matter rather than the name

The idea to produce a business plan sometimes causes cynicism amongst staff. Is it just another imported management fad that someone has picked up on a course? How the process is managed and how people are involved in it has a considerable bearing on the result. An interesting idea to consider is the difference between first order change and second order change. *First order change* is when an organisation can accommodate a change within its manner of working and operating. It adapts and incorporates. *Second order change* is when an organisation has to radically change its way of operating, its culture and style. Many business plans get stuck at first order change. A plan is produced by a few people; it is published, briefly discussed, filed away and quickly forgotten about. This book is concerned not only with producing a credible plan, but also with ensuring that the plan feels real and relevant to people in the organisation. Whether it is called a business plan, a strategic plan or a forward plan is not important.

The dangers of short termism

Political changes, annual budgets and short-term funding can make any notion of planning difficult. Part of thinking strategically is to keep in touch with day-to-day realities and opportunities, but at the same time to focus on future needs and directions. The one thing that is certain is that everything will remain uncertain. Secure and committed long-term funding is doubtful and difficult to achieve. Political and economic stability is unlikely with constant reorganisations, friction between central and local government and a chronic shortage of funds. The profile and expectations of an organisation's users are unlikely to become fixed. There is a real danger of voluntary organisations losing a longer-term perspective, becoming driven by short-term demands and only dealing with what is urgent rather than what is important. Just having a short-term perspective could make a voluntary organisation's existence vulnerable.

During research for this book, a local authority officer with responsibility for grant aiding local voluntary groups said: 'Most of the organisations I deal with would be very easy to cut, and if cut, could close quickly. They are geared up from April to April. They are fearful of taking on longer-term commitments. They employ their staff on short-term contracts (that in practice are often renewed). They have no contingencies. They operate almost as if they expect to be closed down at a moment's notice.'

Management is more and more about accepting uncertainty as a norm and having the confidence to chart a longer-term direction.

Good planning builds on what you do already

All too often, plans degenerate into a 'wish list' of how we would like things to be in a perfect world. The frameworks and ideas suggested in this book aim to ensure that any plan takes into account the realities of the organisation in its present situation. You need to make sure that the plan is realistic and sets out clear steps for its implementation. Too often business plans consist only of catchy mission statements without any real evidence that the organisation has worked out how to move forward.

Making the case for the organisation

Often a voluntary agency suffers from a credibility gap. The outside world sees it as being made up of well-intentioned amateurs. Funders insist on rigorous and bureaucratic controls on how 'their' money is being spent. Sometimes this rubs off on the staff and volunteers who fail to see fully the effectiveness and efficiency of their efforts or that they are achieving incredible results with minimal resources. A central part of a business plan is to make the case for the organisation. It sets out the track record of the organisation, demonstrates that it has effective systems, people and processes in place and that it can deliver results. Voluntary organisations are increasingly being called upon to show (often through producing a business plan) that they will be a reliable partner in a contract or funding agreement. The process of drawing up a business plan often helps an organisation to value itself more and to be more 'assertive' with the outside world.

The planning process in outline

Stage 1: *clarification of the vision and values of the organisation* is about ensuring that there is a clear sense of direction and agreement about the core values that unite an organisation. The decisions reached at this stage should act as an anchor for the rest of the process. Chapter three suggests how an organisation can renew its overall purpose, considers the dangers of simply being driven by what was done in the past and gives some practical hints on drawing up a mission statement.

Stage 2: *an analysis of the current position* is an attempt to take stock of the organisation to date. Chapter four looks at ways of collecting and analysing information about the organisation's current activities, its financial and its management performance, and also suggests ways of predicting how services might develop. It looks at the external environment, and considers how future trends and events might impact on an organisation's future. **Chapter five** reviews the financial information that is needed to plan accurately. It looks at ways of costing work, managing cash flow and the strategic management of finance.

Stage 3: considers how to use this information *to identify key assumptions, strategic choices and direction.* This stage discussed in **chapter six** is a critical one. Informed by a review of internal and external trends, key people in the organisation need to identify choices open to them, evaluate them and agree a direction. This is often a painful process as it usually involves saying what an organisation will stop doing or will not get involved in.

Stage 4: *is about agreeing future strategic direction.* This involves making realistic choices about the future and creating a coherent plan. **Chapter six** suggests several processes for developing strategy.

Stage 5: *making sure that you can achieve the plan and meet its costs* is about the feasibility of planning. **Chapter six** also looks at how to work from the priorities agreed in the previous stage, draw up clear objectives for each one and identify the organisational and management processes needed to meet the plan.

Chapter seven suggests various sources of evidence that an organisation can use in its plan and shows how this information can be used to persuade funders and others to back the organisation.

Chapter eight gives guidance on writing a plan and provides a template and contents list for a plan.

Chapter nine demonstrates the importance of making sure that the plan is implemented, looks at how it can be used to steer and change the organisation and suggests how managers can use, monitor and update the plan.

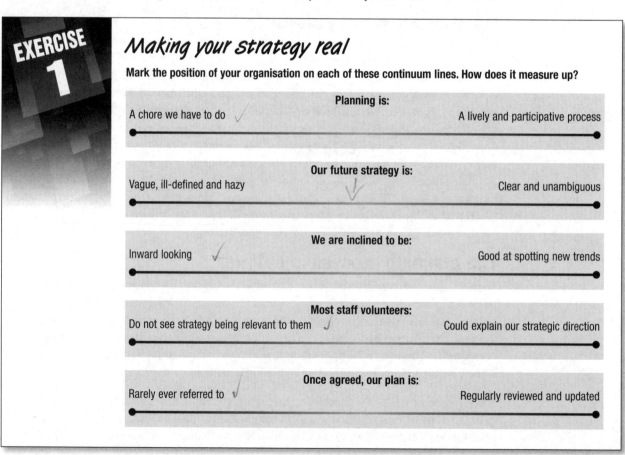

EXERCISE 1

Making your strategy real

Mark the position of your organisation on each of these continuum lines. How does it measure up?

Planning is:

A chore we have to do ———————————————————— A lively and participative process

Our future strategy is:

Vague, ill-defined and hazy ———————————————————— Clear and unambiguous

We are inclined to be:

Inward looking ———————————————————— Good at spotting new trends

Most staff volunteers:

Do not see strategy being relevant to them ———————————————————— Could explain our strategic direction

Once agreed, our plan is:

Rarely ever referred to ———————————————————— Regularly reviewed and updated

EXERCISE 2

Different reasons for business planning

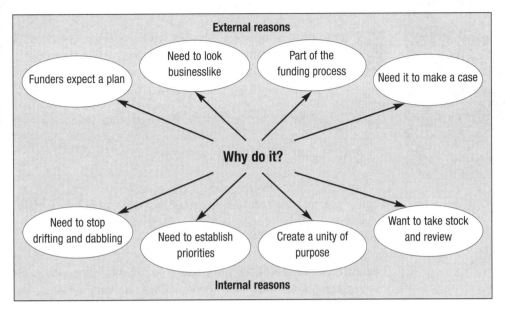

Which of these reasons are important to you? In the boxes provided, score them on a scale of 1 (no or little importance) to 4 (very important):

External

Funders expect a plan:

A good plan helps to make the case for the organisation. It helps funders to understand the organisation and feel confident about backing and supporting it. It "sets out your stall".

Need to look businesslike:

Voluntary organisations need to show that they are properly managed. A business plan can show that there is good and efficient management in place that will ensure delivery and that funds are properly used.

Part of the funding process:

The plan is one of the ways of marketing the organisation. It can explain the idea, vision and strategies to funders and others.

Need it to make a case:

The plan can show how ideas and aspirations can be turned into a reality. It helps people to understand the context and background.

Internal

Need to stop drifting and dabbling:

It is easy to get pulled in many directions at once. A good business plan will help to create clarity about direction and ensure that the organisation is realistic.

Need to establish priorities:

Everything cannot be equally important. Organisations need to decide where and how to focus their efforts – this will include saying 'no' to some ideas, opportunities and requests.

Create a unity of purpose:

The process can bring trustees, staff and volunteers together. Building a shared vision of what we want to do and the strategy for doing it can be a valuable team-building exercise.

Want to take stock and review:

A future plan needs to be based on an appraisal of what you do now. The plan can provide an opportunity to challenge how you do things, evaluate programmes and do a rethink.

You need to balance the internal and external reasons for doing the plan.

Too much emphasis on the external reasons can lead to a plan that is really only written to 'get money out of funders'. Too much emphasis on internal reasons can lead to the process being too inward looking.

Starting the process

The process by which the plan is developed and prepared has a critical impact on its successful implementation. Practical experience consistently shows that the sooner that people potentially affected by change are involved in the planning process the more likely it is that change will be implemented and followed through.

In planning, there is a tendency for a few select individuals to isolate themselves from others, produce a detailed plan written in an inaccessible 'management speak' and then become frustrated when no-one takes the plan seriously.

> 'The finest plans are often spoilt by the pettiness of those who are supposed to carry them out, since even emperors can do nothing without the support of their soldiers.'
>
> Bertolt Brecht

However, it often seems that the greater the number of people involved, the harder it is to manage the process. Meetings become longer, difficult decisions are avoided, the process gets delayed and innovation is strangled by so-called consultation and consensus.

The three levels of the process

One way to resolve this problem is to think of the process as having three levels.

1 A top-led direction setting out boundaries and criteria for the plan.

Trustees and managers need to agree the mission and core values. They need to set a broad organisational context for the plan. This level is about steering a direction for the rest of the plan.

2 Direct input from front line workers and volunteers.

People working in the organisation should be able to contribute and participate in the 'big picture' discussions about mission and values. Once these have been set they should then be able to develop specific plans for their unit or section in the light of the overall direction.

3 Lateral team working both inside and outside the organisation.

Groups of staff, users and committee members can work together to carry out specific aspects of the process such as identifying future trends or exploring possible future scenarios for the organisation.

The whole process of involvement, consultation and participation needs to be tightly managed. If not, the process will quickly degenerate into endless meetings and many bold ideas will be killed by unmanaged consultation.

Careful timetabling, effective delegation of responsibilities and external help with the process may well be needed.

What's up for consultation?

The trustees of Westbury Foundation started their strategic planning process by being very clear about their consultation process. The Chair of the trustees explained how 'the Foundation had drifted. We got involved in far too many issues. After much soul searching the trustees decided that all future programmes had to focus on young people aged 14 to 22.'

'Working with young people had been the original intention – other projects had got added on. After much debate in the organisation the trustees agreed to limit our role to work with young people. We then asked our staff to develop their ideas and come up with some relevant projects that we could run.'

'We made it absolutely clear that the decision to target young people was closed and not up for discussion. However, we wanted the maximum input from staff about how best to work with young people. This was an important break with the past. Often staff were "consulted" on things that had already been decided – a sure recipe for conflict and cynicism. This time we were clear what was and was not up for discussion.'

Managers need to take the responsibility for setting out the direction for the organisation, agreeing key priorities and ensuring that the plan is produced to time and in a cohesive format.

The detailed implementation of the strategy, the production of specific or tactical plans, or the feasibility studies of a project is often best delegated to the people who will have to work on it (and therefore know most about it).

Managers need to ensure that what they produce is in line with the overall strategy of the plan, is realistic, challenging and achievable.

It might also be feasible to involve people who do not directly work in the organisation. Users, carers, supporters and even funders might bring valuable insights and prevent an organisation becoming complacent or inward looking. External consultants can also be engaged to help with the process.

Seeing 'a bit of the jigsaw'

A long-established worker in a health agency was heard describing how his organisation worked to a new worker.

'There are three types of people here. There are a few people at the top – they tell me that they are engaged in "blue sky thinking". They are the "strategists". They spend their time turning out policies and plans. Don't ask them about the day to day service or funding – they are too busy being strategic for that.'

'Then there are the people who deliver the work to our clients. They have to cope with meeting client needs and whatever bright ideas the first lot of people choose to drop on them.'

'The third type are the fundraisers – they have to bring in the money to keep it running and also find new funding for whatever new idea has been dreamed up.'

Although cynical this experience does illustrate a problem.

- As organisations grow, functions get put into compartments. Management can become divorced from service delivery. Functions such as finance and fundraising become remote.

- People only see their bit of the jigsaw. Few see the whole issue.

- Often the internal organisation is dominated by communication gaps and conflicts. Subcultures develop. People have a stronger loyalty to their project or function than to the whole organisation.

Seeing the whole picture

For an organisation to be effective at strategy a style of work or culture needs to develop that encourages people to see the whole picture and how their work fits in.

The following five ideas can help to build this:

Helping everyone to see how they fit in

Try to ensure that the plan answers questions such as 'so, what will this mean for me?' Ensure that the language and style of the plan is based in the real life language of the organisation.

Building in flexibility

Encourage people to go beyond their usual role. Encourage people to participate in project teams or to cover for colleagues. Working flexibly can encourage people to see things differently and gain another perspective.

Breaking down compartmental thinking

Get people to look outside their box. Project staff are only interested in their project, fundraisers do not see the results of their work and administrative staff have little contact with the direct user. Avoiding compartmental thinking needs constant effort. Staff need to be able to see their work in a wider context and also see how their effort is meant to contribute to the broader outcome.

Support learning

Encouraging people to learn new skills and expertise can help the planning process. Involvement in learning might highlight ideas and developments that can be taken forward into the plan.

Work back from the user

Encourage staff to talk to the organisation's users. How is the user base changing? What are their needs and expectations? What do they really need? A refocus on the user can sometimes help people to see the bigger picture.

Getting the process right

A common issue in voluntary organisations is balancing the need to involve people in the planning process and the need to get the plan done. Often consultation and participation can drag on with endless meetings and long-winded attempts to gain a consensus. Alternatively, if people are not actively involved they are unlikely to feel a sense of commitment to the plan.

CASE STUDY

Two approaches at producing a business plan

A housing project had two different experiences of producing a business plan. Its first attempt, motivated simply because the Housing Corporation requested it, was the product of hard labour by the director and the finance manager working together. Few people ever referred to the plan or felt that they had any connection to it.

The next attempt was different. A joint team made up of two committee members, the director, the finance manager and one person from each of the project's three teams produced a mission statement and carried out a review of internal and external developments. The next management committee agreed a brief paper from the director setting out likely assumptions and suggesting five core priorities. For the next six weeks the three work teams had to draw up and cost detailed

and measurable plans for their team's work. The director's role was to act as a coach for them in this process, sometimes pushing them further, but often making sure that they were being realistic. The final plan was produced by a small team led by the finance manager.

The project's director commented that his role had 'been more about thinking about the big picture than about the detail. I had to "hold the ring" on the process and make sure that the plan was an integral product produced on time. It was very difficult for me to stand back and not take the plan over. Two early benefits have been that people now do refer to how their work fits into the plan; and each team now has a work plan which they monitor, but feel a commitment to as they were the main force in setting it.'

A lot depends on organisational culture and style. Often staff have deep-rooted expectations that they should be fully involved in decision-making and that everything is 'up for discussion'. One manager observed, 'if our office caught fire the expectation would be that I would call a staff meeting to discuss how people felt about leaving the building!'

At the start of the planning process it is useful to be clear about the process, how and when decisions will be made and the opportunities for involvement.

The following continuum can help to design the process.

Planning as a process

Level 1		Manager draws up the plan and then informs staff of it.	Clear, quick and simple. Relevant in urgent or contentious situations.	Hard to win commitment to the plan.
Level 2		Manager asks for any views from staff and then draws up the plan.	Slightly more involvement.	Are staff genuinely listened to?
Level 3		Active consultation. Manager leads a series of discussions to consult staff.	Ideas and insights from staff might make the plan stronger.	Can drag on. Often consultation is tokenistic.
Level 4		Consensus. All parties are actively encouraged to reach an agreement.	Can create strong buy in and ownership.	Can be time consuming and also can gloss over conflict.
Level 5		Delegation. Work plans are delegated to individual staff or teams.	Staff are likely to deliver on objectives that they have drawn up.	Objectives must be challenging and fit with overall strategy.

Details of the process

Plan how to plan
Try to pick a good time in the organisation's calendar to work on the plan. People need to have the time to participate in the process.

Identify what is open for consultation
The credibility of the whole process can be easily undermined if people find out that they are being consulted on something that has already been agreed.

Manage time
It is important to ensure that the process does not drift. Often a consultation process can drag on and on. A timetable should be agreed that indicates what should be happening at each stage and when decisions will be made.

Support the process
It might be useful to involve external people to facilitate and guide the process. Consultants can play a valuable role in leading the process and providing an objective and external viewpoint. However, the plan must be owned by the organisation.

Be clear about decision-making

The process must come to an end. This might mean having to draw a line under discussions and debate and come to a conclusion. People need to know when and who will make final decisions on the plan.

Agreeing objectives for the plan

Often there is a lack of confidence or cynicism about the planning process. Most of us have had enough experience of plans that create paper and lead to no action. One starting point is to agree some objectives for the business planning process itself. The task of agreeing these objectives might help to clarify the internal and external reasons why a plan is needed and create an opportunity to measure its value in time.

Although it is probably much better to work out your own possible objectives for business planning, they might include:

- to clarify long-term aims;
- to relate all activities to the aims;
- to develop a realistic future strategy;
- to make measurable plans;
- to link future developments in the external environment to internal change;
- to convince financial backers that the organisation is credible.

A starting point for the process itself is to deal with the often held belief that strategic planning is impossible. The management writer Henry Mintzberg talks about how all organisations are moving in some direction even if they do not know it or have planned it. This is sometimes called an emergent strategy.

CASE STUDY

All organisations are changing all the time

This table shows the 'emergent strategies' of a youth agency i.e. how things change over time.

Trend	Possible cause	Strategic issues
Less outreach work. Now only working with those who come to us.	Pressure of keeping the centre open for ten sessions – funder says that is what is important.	What should be the balance between centre-based and field work?
More in-depth work with fewer young people.	Two workers have trained in counselling and want to practise it.	Is this what we are supposed to be doing?
More young black women using the centre.	Possibly because we employed a woman worker who is black.	What would happen if she left?
More work with 13–16 age group.	Because older ages are into other things.	Who should be our target groups?
More time on fundraising.	Funders will not pay core costs.	Should we find better ways of making our case?
Doing more work on drug misuse.	Because there are funds available for this work.	How could this develop? Do we want to do more or less of this?

A useful exercise is to ask participants in the planning process to think back over the past few years and to try to identify what sorts of direction the organisation has moved in and is currently moving in. Discussion should focus on what has driven the organisation, what has controlled it and what choices have been subconsciously made by individuals and teams.

This exercise can help to illustrate the point that although we cannot always control the detail, the organisation is moving and it is better to chart its path then let it happen by accident.

The language of business planning

Different writers use words like goals, aims and objectives differently. There is no standard textbook definition. The important thing is to ensure that the terms that are used are defined and understood and that they are used consistently.

Planning at three levels – the big picture, the strategic direction and the operational plan

	Key questions	Issues
The big picture	What is the overall vision? What are our core values? How can we measure success?	Can be too vague or unreal? Needs to inspire people to be involved or give support.
Example	'To build a strong and viable local economy that benefits all local people.' Usually a statement of aspiration – setting out a long-term outcome. Often called a mission or vision statement	
The strategic direction	What are our key priorities? What is our direction?	Danger of everything being important. Must be focused.
Example	'We will work to create quality local jobs by offering relevant training and support to local people.' What are you going to do to work towards the vision?	
The operational plan	What do we intend to do and deliver? How do we organise the detail?	Danger of over planning or being too detailed – the plan becomes a 'tick box exercise' or is inflexible.
Example	1. To run six training courses for 350 unemployed local people. 2. To offer learning and basic skills support to all trainees. 3. To carry out an audit of the skills needs of local employers. 4. To develop and pilot a career and training guidance service. Breaking the strategy down into measurable and specific activities. This part of the plan describes what the organisation intends to do and deliver in order to meet the strategy. Linked to available resources and often short term. Sometimes called a delivery plan.	

This book uses four main terms to describe the planning process.

1 *The mission:* This is a brief statement of overall purpose and values. It is the reason why the organisation continues to exist. It says little about what, how, or when an organisation will do something. Mission statements should be a long term statement of intent that follows on from the original vision that inspired the organisation.

2 *Strategic aims:* These set out the direction for the organisation. They are a statement of the key priorities for the organisation in the immediate to medium-term future. Everything the organisation does should be related back to a strategic aim.

3 *Operational objectives:* These are detailed, costed and timed plans of what the organisation will do under each strategic aim. They set out a work plan for the organisation.

The planning process in outline

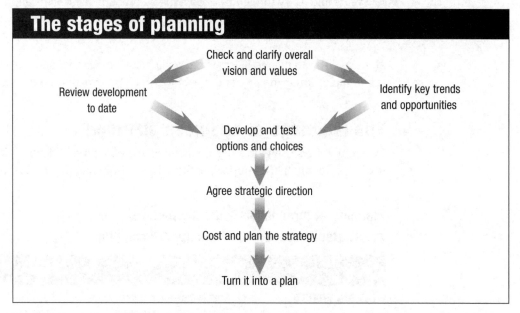

The stages of planning

Check and clarify overall vision and values

Review development to date

Identify key trends and opportunities

Develop and test options and choices

Agree strategic direction

Cost and plan the strategy

Turn it into a plan

The stages of planning laid out above form an outline process map for developing and drafting a business plan.

The order in the process is important.

1 Ensure that there is a clear sense of vision and values before getting involved in the detail.

2 Analyse the organisation's development and identify key external trends as the basis for discussion of future strategy.

3 Agree the strategic direction and then cost the plan.

4 Turn the plan into a document.

The *first stage*, checking and clarifying the overall vision and values, is about answering some fundamental questions:

- What is our overall purpose?
- What are we trying to achieve?
- Who are we for?

Clarity about these questions should provide an anchor for the process.

The *second stage*, the analysis, is two-fold – looking internally at how the organisation has developed and also looking externally to identify how external trends might impact on the organisation. Work at this stage might include gathering and sharing information about the current state of the organisation. This could involve pulling together information about what the organisation does currently and appraising services and activities against the need and purpose. Looking outside the organisation is about trying to predict and anticipate changes that could have an impact on the organisation. The issues identified might be opportunities or threats. Work done at this stage should help to make the planning process a more informed one. It should ensure that before agreeing future direction everyone involved has a sound understanding of the issues facing the organisation both internally and externally.

During this stage, ideas about how the organisation could develop are actively pursued; it should be a creative and challenging time. It is important to encourage fresh and innovative ideas and develop a range of options and choices for future development. Participants should be encouraged to be bold and innovative in their ideas and not be constrained by how things are now or by concerns about funding and resources.

Once the options have been identified they need to be tested. Different tests should be used to consider each option such as:

- does it fit with our mission?
- is it needed?
- are we best able to do it?

The *third stage*, agreeing the strategic direction, is about deciding which options to carry forward and agreeing what will be the organisation's priorities. At this stage decision-making must be clear. All too often people avoid saying 'no' to an interesting or worthwhile idea. Another priority is added in. Critical elements of this stage are:

- agreeing what the organisation is not going to do as well as what it is going to do;
- ensuring that the number of priorities is realistic;
- balancing existing work and new work.

Once the strategy has been agreed the detailed planning work can start. Each service or project needs to be fully costed. The costs involved in properly managing the organisation also need to be added on. Once the costs have been agreed they need to be compared against agreed, likely and possible income. This process usually requires some adjusting of the plan to fit with income projections. This stage also needs to look at the organisation's ability to deliver the plan:

- how might the structure or people's roles need to change to better support the strategy?
- what skills and expertise do we need?
- do we have the management systems and processes to minimise risk and ensure good practice?

The *fourth stage* is about turning the strategy into a document. The finished plan needs to meet the needs of different audiences. External parties such as potential and existing funders need to get a clear message from the plan that helps them to understand the aspirations and intentions of the organisation and also feel confident in the ability of the organisation to deliver it. Internally, trustees and staff should get from the plan a clear understanding of the organisation's direction and priorities and how they fit in.

Two approaches to strategy

What does strategy mean in your organisation? What sort of strategist are you?

Strategy as programming		Strategy as a creative process
Strategy is about detail.	Emphasis	Strategy is about rethinking our purpose and direction.
A blueprint document that sets out exactly what the organisation intends to do.	Result	An ongoing process that creates a united sense of direction.
Numbers, projections, data and tight objectives.	Content	Evaluation, ideas, reflection and clarity of purpose.
'Top' management set the direction – individuals then write their objectives or work plan.	Process	Everyone participates in reviewing where we are at, looking at trends and developing future goals.
Producing a slick and impressive plan.	Style	A chance to stand back from what we do, rethink and work out how to develop.
Funders want it. Corporate planning. Need to be 'business like'.	Driven by	Need to review and be clear where we are going.
Detailed plans, budgets, work plans and timescales.	Focus	Clarity about our intended direction and how we can best move forward.

Tools and techniques

Throughout this book there are a range of tools and techniques to help to develop the business planning process and also to present ideas and analysis in the plan itself. The techniques can be used in three different ways:

At an individual level to clarify thinking and to start to develop ideas.

In groups – management committee meetings, staff meetings and away days – to involve others in the process.

In the plan itself – the completed exercise can be presented in the plan to show the analysis and thinking that led to the plan.

Name	Page	Objective	Issues raised	Notes
Making your strategy real	6	To find out what strategy means in your organisation. Is planning a valuable process or a chore?	Discussion to focus on how to ensure that it is a creative process.	
Different reasons for business planning	7	To establish reasons for planning. To set objectives for the exercise – how will we know that the plan is a success?	Who are we doing it for? For us or for funders?	
How to do it	18	Quick exercise to plan the process – who needs to be consulted?		
Is there a need for strategic thinking?	26	Aims to identify some of the key strategic issues that the plan needs to focus on.		
Working out a mission statement	27	Series of questions and prompts to help to craft a mission statement		
What if we did not exist?	28	To focus on the purpose and the role.	Focus on the why we do it, not what we do.	
What roles do you play?	29	To review the different roles an organisation can play.	Useful to look at how the organisation has evolved and what comes next.	Watch out for taking on too many roles and spreading the organisation too thinly.
At what stage is your organisation's development?	42	To assess what stage of development your organisation is at.		
Comparing mission and activity	43	To check that everything that an organisation does fits with the vision.	Focus discussion on 'how clear is the reason why we do things?'	
Doing a SWOT analysis	44	To provide a snapshot analysis of the issues facing an organisation at a particular point.	Useful way to identify the issues that need to be tackled.	Very well established exercise. Useful as a starter exercise to get people 'identifying the issues'. Good to share different people's perspectives of what are the issues. Needs to be followed up with action planning.
Looking outside – making comparisons	45	To compare the organisation against organisations doing similar work.	What is unique or different about our organisation? What does it do that is special?	The exercise can show how the organisation fits with other services. Also identifies possible co-operation, joint ventures and mergers.

Name	Page	Objective	Issues raised	Notes
Predicting future trends and developments	46	To start the planning process by looking at outside developments, trends and external factors.	May need some research into what are trends.	
A portfolio matrix for your organisation	47	To analyse the value of the different activities or projects of an organisation.	How are different projects developing? Do we have the right balance of activities?	Useful to discuss the criteria by which each activity is valued and also what are the factors that make an activity succeed or fail?
A trading venture checklist	64	To check that the ideas behind a trading venture have been fully worked out and to identify areas for further consideration.		
Predicting trends in current income	65	An action planning sheet to look at the make-up of current income and how it might develop.	Discussion on how to diversify income.	
A financial health check	66	To review financial processes, policies and procedures.	Important that this is not just left to the treasurer.	
Identifying the assumptions behind the plan	82	To identify the assumptions behind the plan.	Are they valid? What happens if they do not work out as planned?	
How clear is the direction?	83	To review how clear the strategy is – useful to do before writing the plan or explaining it to others.		
When did you last have a new idea?	84	To encourage and review innovation.		
Scenario planning	86	To provide an introduction to scenario planning.		
Strategy planner	87	A one page sheet to clarify the measures, actions and costs involved in a strategic goal.		
Strategy prompt worksheet	88	Aims to encourage individuals to identify strategic issues in their area of work.	Ensure that ideas are fed into the planning process.	
Proving your track record	95	A checklist of evidence to show that the organisation has capacity to deliver.		
Putting the plan together	99	To provide a template for drafting the plan.		
The elevator test	101	Quick exercise to check that everyone understands and can put forward the key messages of the plan.		
Evaluating your plan	102	A final check to assess the plan.		

EXERCISE
3

How to do it

Use the table to consider:

- who will give final approval to the plan?
- who will need to be consulted?

Who	What can they bring to the process?	Issues to involve them on?	Best ways of involving them?

What are we about?

Almost all voluntary organisations will have a written constitution which says something about their aims, purpose or goals. What is written in the constitution is legally what the organisation is for. This seems a logical starting point for any planning exercise. However, sometimes this is insufficient. Constitutional aims and objectives are often written in a legal or archaic language which may not be comprehensible. Some constitutions are drafted to allow a broad range of possible activities within a legal structure. Some were written so long ago that they do not 'feel' as if they have anything to do with the organisation.

Recently, mission statements have become increasingly popular as management tools. Perhaps it all started with probably the best known mission statement, that of the USS Enterprise on television's *Star Trek*: 'To boldly go...'

Many organisations have invested time in producing catchy expressions of their purpose. Often the process generates a degree of cynicism. The statement is often little more than a vague slogan, or it has all the certainty of a New Year's resolution.

Two other bits of jargon

Mission creep
Often as a result of chasing funding an organisation finds itself going beyond its core purpose and role. New and different forms of work creep in.

Mission drift
If an organisation does not keep an eye on its core purpose it can easily drift. The organisation takes on too many things. It dabbles in areas of work beyond its original brief. It loses its identity and expertise.

Sometimes the term 'mission' is met with scepticism. It is seen as being a trendy idea and a quick fix technique. Management trends and fads never seem to stop. Some management 'experts' now talk of 'mission drift', when an organisation has stopped following its original mission and started dabbling in other activities and sidelines.

There is a strong argument for ensuring that all the people in an organisation have the same sense of purpose and vision. Work spent on defining the mission can have the following benefits:

- It sets out a longer-term perspective.
- It can create unity around a common vision and identity.
- It makes it clear to both insiders and outsiders what the organisation is about and what it isn't about.
- It creates an overall sense of purpose from which strategy and action can follow.

Discussion of mission and vision can also cause tension and conflict. Some voluntary organisations have become very good at pretending to be all things to all people.

It is not unusual to find different people in the organisation having very different ideas about what is important and what the organisation's priorities should be. Does a community advice centre exist to inform people of their rights? Or to encourage self help? Or to campaign for social change? Or to counsel people with problems? It may well be possible to do all of these things successfully for a period of time. But, when it comes to making decisions about future priorities, future targets or future direction, it is important to have a common view of the organisation's purpose and priorities. If the organisation pretends to do everything, it could well end up fragmented and overstretched.

Three activities are useful for discussing and arriving at a common view:

- identifying what drives the organisation;
- identifying what is (or should be) unique about the organisation;
- describing the organisation's work in terms of outcomes rather than activities.

Mission drift

The Dalston Carers Project was established with the specific aim of providing support to people who cared for a family member or neighbour at home. Its focus was on the carer rather than the person being cared for. The project developed a package of support services for carers to enable them to carry on caring.

The project was very effective, well used and popular. The Council's Social Services Department was so impressed with the project's quality assurance procedures and its overall management that it approached the Project Manager to sound her out about

taking over the management of an elderly people's day centre and a volunteer home visiting scheme.

The project manager explained the management committee's dilemma. 'Our constitutional objectives are sufficiently vague enough to have allowed us to take on these services. It was also flattering to be asked. However, we felt that both of these activities, although needed, would have taken us away from our core business of supporting carers and changed us into being another social care agency. We politely declined.'

What drives the organisation?

Voluntary organisations are driven by other things than simply making money. With many voluntary organisations run largely or even entirely by paid staff, the term 'voluntary' may come to feel less and less relevant. The term 'not for profit' is often used instead. It seems odd to describe an organisation by what it does not aim to do rather than what it is for!

In an organisation there are usually lots of different things driving it at the same time. One way of looking at it is to identify three possible driving forces:

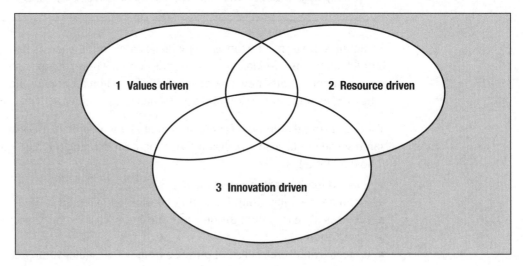

Values driven

The values-driven element is the sense of commitment and shared understanding that holds the organisation together. Values are important in creating a sense of common vision and purpose. However, too much attention to values could lead to the organisation becoming so 'pure' and inward looking that very little ever gets done. Values on their own do not pay people's wages.

Resource driven

The resource element is the capacity of the organisation to fund and staff its activities. Sometimes this is a drive to get bigger and expand by attracting more and more resources, although there is now a growing recognition that just because an organisation is getting bigger it does not mean that it is any more effective.

Innovation driven

The innovation element is the organisation's capacity to innovate, take risks and be creative. Many voluntary organisations came into existence to do things that a public sector agency or private company would not regard sensible practice or too dangerous to invest funds in. Over time, organisations often become safer places and start to reject ideas and innovations that could challenge the status quo. Innovative organisations can be exciting, dynamic and fun. They can also be chaotic, crisis driven and place considerable stress on individuals.

Some questions that emerge from this exercise are:

- What currently drives your organisation?
- Which of these factors do you think is most important?
- How do you manage to combine all the three elements together?
- Which of these are going to be important for the organisation's future?

What is unique about the organisation?

In a commercial organisation a common marketing technique is to identify a product's unique selling proposition or USP. In simple commercial terms it is what makes one washing powder different from another. The difference can be a tangible one (it performs better) or a matter of perception ('it feels right for me').

It is an interesting exercise to pose the question 'what is unique about our service' and to try to list the factors that make the organisation distinctive. What would happen if the services were discontinued or the organisation ceased to exist? Would any alternatives be available? Would clients be better or worse off? Would the organisation have to be reinvented?

Some business organisations have formed their mission statement around the characteristics and factors that make them distinct from other competitors in their market. Work on its 'uniqueness' often helps an organisation to develop a strong sense of identity that holds it together internally and clarifies its purpose externally.

Avoiding a goal

Six reasons why not-for-profit agencies often find clear goal definition elusive.

- The fear of accountability. Having a clear goal increases the visibility of managers. They become more accountable.

- Many organisations continue to have projects when they no longer serve the goal. Winding an activity up can be very painful, so something which accomplishes little is allowed to continue.

- Taking on an activity because money is available. The availability of funding becomes the driving force, not goals or needs.

- A fear that management science may replace romance: 'Won't hard nosed evaluation undermine humanitarian instincts?'

- A lot of time in voluntary agencies is spent on tasks which do not fit into any identifiable goal. Servicing meetings, encouraging goodwill, liaison with other bodies, public relations and meeting requests for information all make it easy for the organisation to be distracted from its mission.

- That the financial indicators that a profit making company has are less meaningful in a voluntary agency. They say little about progress towards the goal.

Philip D Harvey and James D Snyder

Reproduced with the permission of the Harvard Business Review

About values

Values are important to a voluntary organisation. Values are:

- the ethos that underpins the organisation's purpose and work;
- the core beliefs that should influence and inform all activities;
- what the organisation stands for.

Agreeing and setting out what an organisation's values are can help an organisation to be successful.

They can create a unifying set of principles for all staff and workers to work to. Strong values can help to build and maintain teamwork.

They can help to develop a distinctive edge for an organisation. The director of an agency working with people with disabilities explained how 'there are something like twenty groups locally working on disability issues. It is the application of our values – of user involvement, participation and respect – that gives us our identity and differentiates us from other groups.'

Values can help guide an organisation's future development. New directions, new opportunities and new ideas should all fit with the organisation's value base.

Examples of values might include:

- ensuring that users have choice;
- valuing difference and diversity;
- willingness to work in collaboration with others.

Values can be problematic. There is a danger of values simply being slogans; it requires committed and sustained management to turn a vague statement like 'putting people first' into an idea that means something for everyone in the organisation. Also some values can be 'taken too far' or produce a negative impact. Does a commitment to participation and consultation mean endless meetings and an inability to ever make a clear and fast decision?

Outcomes and activities

The past few years have seen considerable interest in the terms outputs and outcomes. Policymakers and funders talk of taking an 'outcome approach'. Managers spend their time struggling to find ways of recording or proving outcomes. Discussion of outcomes can be a very useful way of clarifying the mission or purpose of an organisation. A simple model is often used to explain the concept.

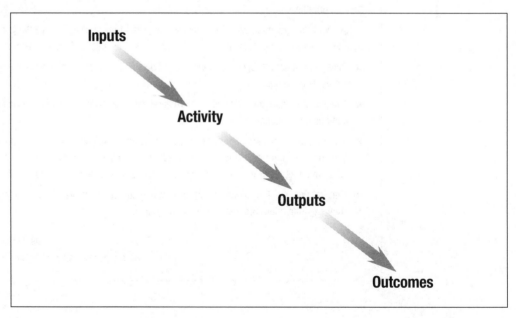

Inputs

Activity

Outputs

Outcomes

The inputs are the resources (money, time, people) committed to an activity. Outputs are what the organisation produces or delivers. Examples of outputs include giving advice, running training programmes or providing emergency accommodation. Outcomes are the difference that you make. Some outcomes are about creating a change; others are about preventing something negative from happening. Examples of outcomes include:

- 'Enabling a person to continue to live independently.'
- 'Establishing a self-help group capable of running its own affairs and sustaining itself.'
- 'Stopping a young person getting involved in crime.'
- 'Recruiting and supporting a trained volunteer network.'

Setting up activities and producing outputs without checking on the outcomes is not a productive or sensible use of time and limited resources. Outcomes are hard to identify, often outside of an organisation's direct control and may not be seen for some considerable time. Outcomes are really what an organisation was set up to achieve. However well managed, activities and outputs without outcomes are pointless. As management writer, Peter Drucker said, 'There is nothing so useless as doing efficiently that which should not be done at all.'

CASE STUDY

Catering or care?

The Millhead charity provided meals on wheels for isolated elderly people living alone. The charity had expanded rapidly over the past few years and had appointed a coordinator to lead a dedicated team of staff and volunteers. The coordinator was soon involved in negotiating contracts with social services and producing the never-ending documentation that the social services department demanded.

A year into the post, the coordinator organised a review day with staff, trustees and volunteers. This review session looked at the new quality assurance standards developed at the instigation of social services. They set out various minimum standards about menu choice, food nutrition and catering management. Somehow they did not feel right.

At the end of the session it suddenly occurred to the coordinator that the activity of cooking and delivering food had taken over from the charity's original purpose, to support, care for and befriend isolated elderly people. The means had become the end.

The coordinator explained her feelings to the group. A volunteer explained that what was important to the old people she was delivering meals to was knowing that the same person would visit them every Tuesday and Thursday lunchtime and not how often the menu changed or how healthy the meal was. Another volunteer talked about how for some old people the actual meal was pretty irrelevant; what was important was the five minutes of conversation with the volunteer.

After the session the coordinator worked on a business plan that stressed that what the charity valued was personal care and time with elderly people. These aims could be delivered in several ways such as home visiting, good neighbour schemes or helping relatives to visit more often as well as delivering food.

The mission statement shifted the focus from providing a catering service to a service providing individual care and contact delivered through a variety of activities.

Most organisational systems such as job titles, job descriptions and structures are geared around the activity rather than the outcome. Often the energy needed to keep the activity going can start to obscure the outcome. Giving advice, providing a day centre and running a training centre are descriptions of activity and not outcome.

A useful starting point in a planning process is to agree what are the kinds of outcomes that the organisation wants to create.

- What outcomes do we wish to achieve?
- How will we know if we achieve the outcome?
- What are the activities that will help us achieve the outcome?

Drawing up a mission statement

Informed by work on what drives the organisation, what makes it unique and what outcomes are important, you should now be able to produce a short mission statement for your organisation that sets out its purpose.

CASE STUDY

A misguided mission

The director of a regional museum did not expect much discussion when he tabled his draft 'mission statement' at the quarterly trustees' meeting. The trustees were mainly academics or amateur historians who had little time for management ideas.

The draft described the mission as:

'To be a lively, open and popular educational experience. To display our collection in a creative and exciting way. To ensure that the museum is open and accessible to local people.'

The chair of the trustees expressed concern that there was no mention of scholarly pursuits or of preserving the museum's collection for common heritage. One trustee said that the mission statement would be more suited to a theme park rather than a centre for study and historical research.

The director thought back over previous trustees' meetings. There had been some criticism of his proposal to recruit a marketing officer rather than fill a vacant curator's post. Another disagreement was over spending money on a schools' education pack rather than on extending the collection. The trustees showed no interest in his performance measures which showed a steady rise in visitors, they only seemed concerned with the academic credentials of the staff and the quality of the collection.

At the end of the meeting, the director agreed to redraft the mission statement in the light of the discussion. No doubt, he would be able to come up with a compromise set of words that would meet his desire to have a lively and popular museum and the trustees' concern for academic excellence.

Three questions worried him.

Would the compromise wording work in practice or was he just avoiding a fundamental difference which should be resolved in a more substantial way?

Was it possible to 'direct' an organisation where people were being asked to face in different directions?

Could the two approaches be brought together or would the conflict boil leading to confusion?

Good mission statements:

- are short – no more than forty words;
- are focused on the value to the user and the relationship with the user;
- set out the overarching goal of the organisation;
- describe the values that will influence how that goal will be achieved.

Mission statements do not need to be measurable, specific or targeted. A mission statement by itself is useless. Once agreed it must be followed up by a clear strategy for the organisation and focused objectives for its work.

Why bother with missions and visions?

Here are six reasons why it is useful to spend time ensuring that the mission is clear:

A good mission holds an organisation together

The mission statement should help people to understand what the organisation is trying to achieve or change. It should stress the 'ends' rather than the 'means'.

A strong mission should convey the core values

As well as saying what the organisation is for it should also highlight the core values and ethos that should influence and underpin all that the organisation does. This can help to build a strong and dynamic organisational culture.

It gives criteria to judge ideas and possible projects against

All activities, services and projects should fit with the mission statement. An important test for a new idea or a new proposal should be that it fits with the organisation's mission.

(continued)

Why bother with missions and visions? (continued)

It gives focus to an organisation

The mission should give a longer-term view. It should help people to see their work in a broader context and help people to understand the point of each person's contribution.

It makes clear the boundary and limits of the organisation

The mission statement should stop the organisation taking on activities that take it beyond its remit and role.

It makes clear what is different about the organisation

The mission should make the organisation's particular distinctive characteristics clear. Lots of agencies work with the same client group – in what way are you different?

What roles do we play?

Once the mission is agreed it is then useful to look at what roles the organisation can best play to meet the mission. Often organisations take on or assume a role. As organisations develop the number of roles they play can grow.

Typical roles might include the following.

- Advocate – working on behalf of people to influence decisions and policies positively.
- Campaigner – raising public awareness to win support and achieve change.
- Expert – being the recognised expert body.
- Innovator – finding new and effective ways of delivering services.
- Information provider – producing and providing information to the public at large and specific audiences.
- Network organiser – coordinating, supporting and leading individuals and agencies.
- Service provider – managing and delivering direct services to beneficiaries.
- Support role – facilitating and organising support for people with a common interest.
- Educator and trainer – offering programmes to develop skills.
- Research and policy role – monitoring and responding to new policies and practices.

CASE STUDY

Playing different roles

The Heathgrove Network identified an evolution through several roles in its fifteen years' history. The network was established by a group of parents whose children had a drink or drugs problem.

The network's committee could identify three different phases:

Early stages years 1–3	Mature stage years 3–10	Renewal years 11–15
When it started the group's main role was to provide mutual aid and support to parents. In time the group members started to be an advocate to policymakers.	The success of the early stages led to the group having a high profile. It started to win funding and employ staff. By year 5 the network was running an information service, providing direct services and developing new and innovative ways of working with clients. This phase led to organisational expansion and a change in the style and culture of the network.	The renewal phase came after some serious discussions as to the role and purpose of the network. The management committee agreed to focus on three main roles: To be regarded as the lead or expert body. To campaign for better service provision. To educate and train other agencies in how best to work with families.

As Heathgrove evolved through these roles the character and style of the organisation changed. The early stages were informal with an emphasis on mutual self help. In the middle stage the emphasis shifted to delivering services and the third stage was an attempt to develop the influencing and campaigning work. It was interesting to note that the movement into these roles had evolved and never been deliberately planned.

Is there a need for strategic thinking?

The following eight statements were made by a group of managers about to embark on a strategic planning exercise.

Do any of the sentiments expressed sound like your organisation?

1. 'We have grown far too fast. Some parts of the organisation are now disconnected from each other.' N

2. 'We are drifting. The past few years all our energy has been spent on keeping going. We need to establish a new direction.' Y

3. 'We need to establish a common sense of purpose and direction that will hold the project together.' N

4. 'We could be criticised for trying to be all things to all people. We need to sort out our identity and make priorities.' Y

5. 'The need for our services is growing fast, the resources to meet that need is declining. We are in danger of becoming a crisis, 'first aid' service.' Y W

6. 'We have been so busy managing that we have missed out on several opportunities to develop new initiatives.' Y

7. 'I have trouble explaining what the organisation is for to outsiders.' N

8. 'We are in danger of becoming complacent and inward looking. We cannot assume that what we are doing now will be the same in two years' time.' Y

How would you describe the current state of strategic thinking in your organisation?

- Minimal
- Ad hoc
- Self-enforced

Who does it? Where does it happen?

- Mgt / team - volunteer
- Office
  Outreach
  Home Visits

How could it be improved?

- Better supervision
- More skilled volunteers
- appointment system
- Feedback

26

EXERCISE 5

Working out a mission statement

These questions are designed to help you draft a mission statement for your organisation.

Objectives

> What are the objectives and purpose of the organisation as set out in the constitution?

Original aim

> Why was the organisation set up? What was the original idea?

Outcomes

> What outcomes do you want to bring about?

Success

> What would be success for your organisation?

Values and ethos

> What values should influence the organisation?
> What does it stand for?

Difference

> What should be different about the organisation?

Review your answers.

Spot key words or concepts

Use the information to produce a statement of no more that thirty to forty words.

EXERCISE 6

What if we did not exist?

This is a very simple exercise to get people thinking about the purpose and role of their organisation.

If we did not exist:

What would be different?

Who would miss us?

What would be the impact if we did not exist?

Would we have to be reinvented?

EXERCISE 7

What roles do you play?

Role	Current involvement – very high to non-existent	Future perspective	Is it likely to: - increase - decrease - stay the same
Advocate			
Campaigner			
Expert body			
Innovator			
Information provider			
Network organiser			
Service provider			
Support role			
Educator and trainer			
Research and policy role			
Other roles:			

How many roles is it viable to play at one time?

How do these roles fit with our mission?

Analysis

 business plan must include a realistic appraisal of the following.

- Basic management information about the cost of the service and organisational performance.
- A review of likely future trends and scenarios.
- A critical assessment of the organisation's strengths and weaknesses.

The business plan needs to demonstrate that past history and current performance have been properly evaluated to create the best plan for the future. This chapter looks at how organisations can collect and interpret information and feed it into a plan.

"Get the facts first. You can always distort them later."

Mark Twain

What information is needed?

Three types of information are needed to inform and develop the plan.

Information about external developments

The changing state of the organisation's market – i.e. level and type of demand for the organisation's services.

- New ways of working and developments in the sector.
- New needs and types of users.
- Developments in similar agencies.
- Known factors that will demand a response.
- Predicted factors and trends that could require a response.
- The extent of need.

Information about internal developments

- Recognition of key strengths and weaknesses.
- Ideas about how to develop the service.
- The needs and expectations of current users.

Information about the business and financial position

- What services cost to operate.
- How costs compare to other agencies.
- Estimates of future income.
- Break-even and break points.

Using a SWOT analysis to get started

A very well established tool in business planning is a SWOT analysis. It involves participants identifying and recording:

Strengths	Weaknesses
Opportunities	Threats

In a SWOT exercise participants contribute their assessment of the organisation in terms of its strengths and its weaknesses, and their ideas about its future (the opportunities and threats). In using a SWOT the following things often happen.

Three activities are useful for discussing and arriving at a common view:

- People find it easier to identify weaknesses and threats rather than strengths and opportunities. It is often useful to insist that participants identify a minimum number of strengths.
- What some people see as a weakness others may see as a strength. One person might see a day centre as being disorganised, and unprofessional. Another might see it as relaxed, friendly and accessible to the intended client group. Discussion about such different perceptions can be really valuable.
- Often things are neither an opportunity or a threat – they move around in the middle. A new funding regime could 'go either way'; it could be an opportunity or a threat.
- Often discussion time is focused on overcoming the weaknesses. However, it is worthwhile to spend time on the strengths and to focus on what were the factors that created their success.

A SWOT is a good way of capturing the issues facing an organisation and getting the different views of a range of people.

Taking the SWOT further

Once the four elements of the SWOT have been completed it is useful to spot key issues and themes. Discussion needs to move on beyond analysis and look at what actions are needed.

A simple way of doing this is to look at each subject box and ask:

- For the *strengths* what action do we need to consolidate and keep them?

- The *weaknesses* may need some probing – what action is needed to overcome them? Could any of the weaknesses be turned around and become an opportunity?

- The *opportunities* might need some further work or investment?

- The *threats* are often organisational risks – what action is needed to protect the organisation against them?

Moving from analysis to action is a useful way of getting people to identify future strategy and actions.

Predicting external trends

Our ability to predict accurately how things will be is obviously limited. Traditional corporate planners have tried to sift information, analyse issues and forecast the future. They are usually not particularly accurate and often downright wrong! The approach here is more about identifying trends and working out how best to respond. Good strategic management is about being able to respond quickly and effectively to new developments and events.

In all activities there are trends and developments that could shape an organisation's future. A key skill – if not an art – is being able to spot the trend early enough and being able to respond to it in a proactive rather than a reactive way.

Predicting trends and developments

Some of the key future issues for a social charity are set out in this chart.

	Available resources	Changes in how we work	Changes in demand and needs	Changes in the political and economic arena	Changes in the environment or market that we operate in
Next 12 months	Fundraising from public will stand still or decline.	Some services at breaking point if demand continues.		How will community care reforms work in practice and impact on us?	Do we cooperate or compete with similar agencies?
1–3 years	Lease expires on building.	External evaluation of project scheduled.	Impact of recession on users and carers.	Move to a new local authority structure.	Push for a formal quality assurance system.
Longer term	Long-term aim of user control and management.	Our clients will get older...break up of care arrangements. Greater demands for choice and independence.	Voluntary agencies having to take over previous statutory services.	Potential conflict with other providers over values.	

Possible trends might include the following.

- Available resources – what will happen to the different kinds of resources we need to do our work? This could include funding, staff and volunteers and other inputs into the organisation such as goodwill.
- Changes in how we work – new working methods, styles and ways of working with the user. What's new in our sector?
- Changes in demand and need – how might the profile and make-up of our user client base change? How might patterns of demand change? How might needs and expectations change?
- Changes in the political and economic arena – how might new legislation, new political directions and broader social change impact on our work?
- Changes in the environment and market – what is happening to other agencies who we work with?

"The future ain't what it used to be."

Arthur C. Clarke

The trends can be divided into categories.

- Facts – trends that we know will happen.
- Opinions – assessments based on experience of past trends.
- Guesswork – hunches about what might happen.

After listing the trends it is useful to:

- See if any can be grouped together into relevant clusters.
- Decide which ones are going to be key issues or drivers for the organisation.
- Discuss how the organisation can best respond and make it an opportunity.
- Identify first steps.

CASE STUDY

Spotting trends

The staff team of a national health charity identified twenty key trends that could impact on their work and would need to be considered as part of their strategic planning process:

Much greater knowledge about the disease

More media interest

People expect instant information

Greater use of the internet

Some people will not be online

Medical advances – new drugs

Lack of reliable information about drugs

Other agencies doing what we do

Greater competition between charities

Information overload

More legislation likely

Other agencies asking us for information

Greater public awareness

Local groups starting to campaign

Tougher fundraising climate

New ways to fundraise

Some interest from parliamentarians

Some supporters can't/won't join local groups

Offers of sponsorship from drug companies

People want information outside office hours

The team decided to focus on four key issues:

- greater use of technology;
- other agencies getting involved in our work;
- medical developments – new drugs;
- more media interest.

The team felt that these four issues would be critical for the organisation. The issues would need to be high on their agenda. The team decided to look at how the organisation could best respond by looking at the charity's four main areas:

- the network of 30 local groups spread throughout the country;
- the campaign team;
- the information service;
- the fundraising team.

	Greater use of technology	Other agencies getting involved in our work	Medical developments – new drugs?	More media interest
Local groups	Explore ways of networking local groups. Some groups could meet on the web rather than in person.	Potential for collaboration locally. Danger of competition.	Provide regular updates for local groups.	Encourage local groups to appoint volunteer press officers. Provide training and support to volunteer press officers in order to increase local coverage.
Campaign team	Set up an e-campaign group	Could we create a joint agency alliance to lobby government	Carry out research to monitor spending on drugs – is there fairness across the country?	Develop contact with specialist health journalists. Feed them positive stories and ideas for features.
Information service	Shift from paper to electronic communications. Need to work out how we charge for web-based information.	Need to benchmark our information service against others.	Need to produce specialist and up-to-date information on new drugs. Special section on the website.	Can the information service continue to field all press calls? Do we need a full-time press officer?
Fundraising	Must ensure that people can donate online at our website.	Implications for more competition in funding. We need a stronger brand identity.	Drug companies might wish to sponsor our work or advertise in our publications. Need to develop an ethical policy on this.	Fundraising team should build on greater awareness.

Not seeing the obvious

For the Castlerigg charity, commissioning an independent survey of user needs had been a big and expensive issue. The trustees had eventually agreed to contract with an independent researcher to scope the nature of client need and in particular to highlight unmet need. After a tendering process a university department was appointed to carry out a needs review.

Six months later the researchers delivered their report. Whilst photocopying the report one of the charity's general office staff happened glance over

its executive summary. The report did not identify specific gaps in provision. Indeed it recommended further investigation. The charity's office assistant despaired. Why hadn't they just asked her? On an average day a quarter of the calls to the charity's main number were met with 'I am sorry we don't do that.' The general office staff knew more about unmet needs and service gaps than anyone else, but no-one ever recorded or even asked about occasions when people were turned away.

Making comparisons

Another external analysis is to look at how the organisation relates to and fits with other agencies doing similar or related work. This exercise can be useful in identifying potential conflicts or duplication of effort, but more positively to identify gaps in provision and potential for cooperation, alliances and joint work.

The first step in the exercise is to list all the organisations who do (or might be perceived as doing) similar things to your organisation. Few organisations have identical comparators, so list anyone who does some similar things to you.

Once a list has been completed it is useful to compare the key similarities and differences between each agency and yours and then go on to look at the relationship between agencies and how it might develop.

Analysis of the exercise should focus on the following questions.

- What's different or special about what we do compared to the others?
- Can we use what is unique about us to market or promote the organisation?
- How does the map of provision fit together?
- What potential is there for cooperation, joint ventures, alliances and even mergers?
- Do we cooperate or compete?

It is also useful at this stage to look at how other agencies' strategies and policies might have impact on your work. For example a local authority's children's service plan might be useful in identifying opportunities for a local children's project.

Looking outside

A locally-managed housing advice project carried out this exercise to look at how it related to other agencies who did similar work to it. The following chart is a summary of their analysis.

Agency	Similar to us	Different to us	Relationship	Strategic issues
Citizens Advice Bureau	Operates an 'open door' policy. Very busy.	Part of a national service. Strong public profile. Use volunteers.	Good – joint training.	Potential for more joint work.
Law Centre	Very busy.	Appointments only. More specialist.	Lost contact due to staff changes.	Need to re-establish contact.
Housing Aid Centre at the Town Hall	Town centre location.	Only does housing advice. Directly managed by the council.	Poor relationship in the past.	Could we be seen as rivals? Do we overlap? How can we work together?
Solicitors in private practice		They are profit-making. Expensive. Sometimes act for landlords.	Mixed – some good personal relationships.	Could we encourage pro bono work?

Looking at internal issues: reviewing programme lifecycles

The planning process should be an opportunity to take a fresh look at the kind of services and activities the organisation is involved in. This should be a chance to renew and revitalise activities by challenging them and agreeing how they can best develop. The plan needs to show that the organisation has thought critically about its current operation and that given all of its activities some kind of objective appraisal has been done.

An interesting approach is to look at where each activity is on the lifecycle diagram set out below. The different stages are as follows.

Understanding the lifecycle

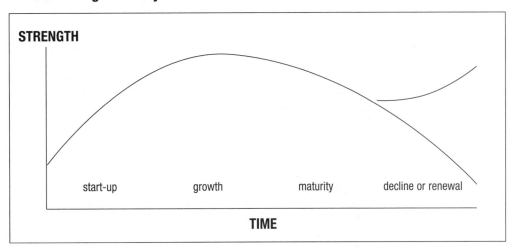

Start-up

The activity is new. It is still trying to establish itself and is hopefully building up its expertise. It is innovative and keen to try new things. This stage involves a lot of hard work and a lot of learning.

Growth

Assuming that the start-up is successful the activity may well grow. It develops more activities and starts to roll out new services to more people. Often success in this stage leads to more opportunities and more work. The profile of the activity is usually high.

Consolidation/mature stage

In this stage the activity is on a plateau. It is delivering services in a safe and reliable way. An element of routine creeps in. Systems become important.

Decline

In this stage there is little energy or innovation left. The activity is inclined to simply repeat what it has always done. It is 'going through the motions'. New work is left for start-up projects. This stage can lead to a fall in quality or crisis.

Renewal

The final stage is about renewal. This usually involves tackling the decline. The activity needs to be re-evaluated and given a fresh focus. Sometimes in this stage an activity needs to be relaunched or brought to a close.

Several issues can be worked on as a result of this model:

- How long does the cycle take? Increasingly organisations are moving through it very fast. Today's 'state of the art' technology will soon be out of date.
- What are the critical issues for each stage? What sort of management style is needed?
- How do we manage decline or closure?

Stages in the development of organisations

	1. Start-up stage	2. Growth stage	3. Consolidation stage	4. Renewal stage
Theme	Innovation Vision led Experimental	Taking on new activities Fast growth	Organisation delivers a range of services often to contract	Rethinking refocusing the organisation
Key issues	Founder centred	Growth through projects	Geared around delivering services	Clarity of purpose
Style	Informal Entrepreneurial Task-led Dynamic	Becoming 'service based' Need to get organised	Need to show the delivery of outputs. 'Businesslike'	Redevelopment of campaigning and advocacy
Funding	Reactive Grab funding	Funding for specific projects. 'Flavour of the month funding'	Mixed funding: grants, contracts and fees	Diversified funding
Organisational issues	Few procedures and policies	Need plans, systems, and measures. Core/project split Specialisms emerge	Are we just another service provider? Management costs rise	Clearer sense of mission, purpose and independence
Management issues	Leadership rather than management	Management systems need to develop	How to hold it all together – more than a collection of projects	Need strong management and leadership

A useful way of planning ahead is to look back at how the organisation has developed and trying to understand its history might give an insight into its future development.

The model set out in the table above aims to describe different stages that many voluntary organisations go through.

- The first stage is the start-up stage. The organisation is driven by a compelling vision of what it wants to achieve or change or by a real energy to get things done. Often in this stage the organisation is led by one or two key individuals who project the vision, hold it all together and set the tone, pace and direction. The organisation lacks procedures and processes. Funding is grabbed as a means to an end. Often this stage is characterised by hard work, energy and creative innovation.

- Movement into the second stage is often driven by successes in the first. The organisation's energy and dynamism attracts people. The organisation expands by taking on new initiatives and projects. Often in this stage the need to be organised (or at the very least legal) is recognised. Rules, policies and procedures are needed to ensure proper services and to meet contractual obligations and funders' expectations.

- The third stage can be characterised by the organisation consolidating, searching for efficiency and being focused on service delivery. Systems, procedures and processes are produced. Often the organisation's core expands. Functions and specialisms such as personnel or fundraising develop. Costs rise as levels of management and administration are added on.

- The fourth stage is about rethinking and refocusing. The organisation needs to revisit its purpose. Possibly it may have expanded and grown away from its original vision. Getting bigger is not enough. The organisation might need to review all its activities to see if they really make a difference to users.

In the movement through these stages several things can happen.

There is disruption. The movement between stages is often gradual but can nevertheless be disruptive. People frequently leave between stages. Individuals who might be very effective at creating a vision, involving others and being innovative in the first stage might not be so good at creating the sound management systems and procedures needed in the later stages as the organisation grows.

A culture clash develops. As an organisation develops and grows its style, atmosphere and informal way of doing things change. One worker described how 'when we started out it was all very informal, everyone mucked in. As the organisation grew it changed. People stopped seeing the whole picture. They were only interested in their own project or bit of the organisation. Fundraisers, admin and project staff all developed their own sub cultures – which at times clashed or at best failed to communicate.'

The funding changes. The organisation's funding mix and relationship to funders change. In the early stages funding is obtained from any available source to start the organisation. A trustee of a new organisation recalled how 'in the early days we grabbed whatever funding was going.' As the organisation develops growth is often through project funding. The organisation wins contracts to deliver certain funds. Often some parts of the organisation get well funded while others suffer. A key issue is how to fund the organisation's administrative and managerial core. The expectations of funders become more explicit. They are commissioning the organisation to *deliver* an output rather than simply *funding* it. The work involved in managing funding increases – funders want to monitor information to ensure performance. In the fourth stage the organisation aims to develop what one manager described as a 'mixed economy' of funding – a mixture of grant aid, service or project contracts plus an element of earned income through developing forms of trading or charging for some services.

The skill basis changes. Often new skills are needed in the move from one stage to another. The entrepreneurial skills needed to turn an idea into an organisation, win funding support and inspire others to be involved are different from the organisational management skills needed in the second and third stages. In these stages the emphasis is on implementing systems, planning, controlling resources and ensuring that the organisation is legally compliant, has proper policies and procedures and can deliver consistent service.

A portfolio analysis

The Boston Consulting Group developed a useful business tool for companies, to enable them to look at their various products and services as a portfolio matrix. With a little adaptation it can be applied to voluntary organisations that offer several projects and services.

The matrix is made up of four squares as shown below.

2 stars	1 question marks
3 cash cows	4 dead dogs

Square one: the question marks. Question marks are projects and activities that are still being developed. They could become a star. They take up resources, but as yet are not fully delivering. Question marks could be a start-up project, a pilot activity or even an idea that is being developed.

Square two: the organisational stars. These activities are currently particularly strong and may have potential for growth. They are dynamic, popular and creative. Some stars are short lived 'shooting stars'.

Square three: the cash cows. Cash cows are reliable and mature services and activities. They operate well and often provide a degree of stability in the organisation. There is a danger of cash cows being ignored or taken for granted.

Square four: the dead dogs. These activities take up time and resources, but produce little of value in return.

From working this model, several strategic options and choices can be identified.

What criteria are being used? In a profit-making venture the criterion is usually a simple one of 'is it bringing in a profit?' A voluntary organisation might need to agree the importance of different criteria – does it produce outcomes? Is it what our users want? Is it creative?

What should be the balance? How do we balance being risky and innovative (running stars and question marks) and the need for stability (cash cows). How do we get a balanced portfolio? How much time do we put into developing new ideas into projects that will replace the dead dogs?

How do activities move through the matrix? Today's dead dogs might well have been last year's stars. Are we really evaluating and planning our work? What are the factors that make things work?

Strategic questions to ask about the activities placed in each box are:

Question marks

- How long does it need to prove itself?
- How will we know that it is working and is a success?
- How prepared are we to manage some risk and failure?

Stars

- What makes it a star?
- Can we replicate these factors elsewhere?
- Where will it go next?

Cash cows

- For how long can we assume that this activity will stay stable?
- Do we take it for granted?

Dead dogs

- Should we close it down or reinvest effort in it?
- Why has it been left in this box?
- What options do we have?

CASE STUDY

Youth Development Agency – portfolio matrix

Square 2 stars	Square 1 question marks
Counselling Helpline *Disability Youth Group*	*Health project* *Computer project*
Square 3 cash cows	Square 4 dead dogs
Centre-based clubs *Arts project* *Sports activities*	*Residential centre* *International Exchange*

Square 1 had two new projects. First, a health project that was still very much at a pilot stage. No-one knew if it would work, but it was considered worth investing in. Second, the computer project. This project had been around the organisation for two years. It had attracted little interest from users (or funders) and really was little more than the 'pipe dream' of a particular worker.

Square 2 consisted of two new projects that were 'breaking new ground' locally, picking up considerable media interest and getting a very good response from young people with whom the project had traditionally had very little relationship. One of the projects, the counselling line, was also attracting interest from a neighbouring local authority who expressed an interest in developing a similar service.

Square 3 took up most of the organisation's resources. They were the main activities that operated on a week-to-week basis. Over the past five years they had changed little and as far as the organisation was concerned would continue to serve a useful purpose. One of the activities, the arts project, was causing concern. It was starting to drift. It was attracting fewer young people. Its funder had described it as 'becoming rather predictable'.

Square 4 had two activities that were part of the agency's history. The residential centre, a cottage, was donated to the agency ten years ago. At that time it was, for a short period, a 'star'. For the past two years, it had needed considerable repairs, a new roof and regular visits from the agency's administrator. As a result, it drained resources and because of the poor state of repair few groups ever visited. The international exchange programme had become an annual commitment that the agency did because it had 'done it last year'. Few people participated, it often went over budget and took up considerable staff time. However, those who did participate thought that it was very valuable.

The portfolio analysis highlighted six strategic choices for the agency.

1 Innovation was seen as an important role for the agency. How much time and money could it risk in square 1? How much time should it give new ideas to establish themselves?

2 What future is there for the two items in square 2? Could they peak? What if funders lost interest (moved onto other stars), but expectation from users continued to rise?

3 Are we really confident that the items in square 3 are steady and safe?

4 What do we need to do with the arts project? How do we stop it drifting into square 4?

5 What future do we envisage for the residential centre? Do we invest in it, market it and give it a new direction or do we look to dispose of it?

6 Should we continue with the international exchanges? If we move out of this area will we get opposition from those of our members who benefit from it? Could we float it off to someone more skilled in this area?

Reviewing the operation of the organisation

Part of the analysis needs to look at how the organisation is organised and operates. Questions to consider include the following.

- Is the organisation flexible enough to respond to changes and uncertainties?
- Does the way we are organised and work fit with our values and what we want to do?
- Do all aspects of the organisation fit together?

The management consultancy firm Mckinsey & Company developed a useful framework for taking stock of an organisation. They argue that for an organisation to be effective it has to achieve a synergy between seven elements, all of which helpfully begin with the letter S.

The 7-S framework

The 7-S framework (see below) can be used to identify weaknesses and shortcomings in how an organisation works.

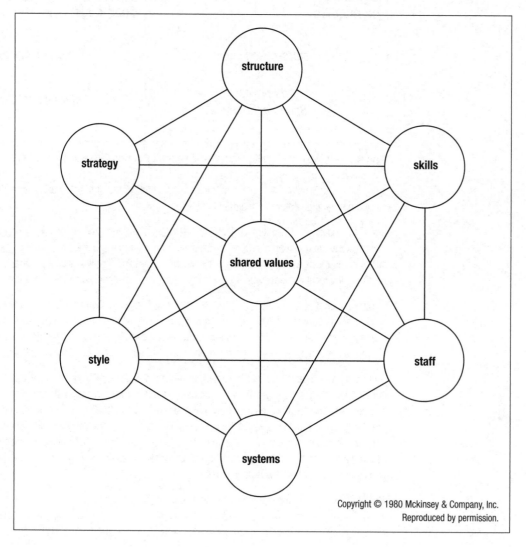

Copyright © 1980 Mckinsey & Company, Inc.
Reproduced by permission.

Strategy

- Does the organisation have a clear purpose?
- Is it future orientated?
- Do people in it understand its strategy?

Structure

- Does the way that work is divided up make sense?
- Is the structure flexible enough?
- Does it allow good communication between people?

Staff

- Are the right sort of people in the right sort of jobs?
- What sort of employer are we?

Skills

- Do we have the right skills mix to develop in the way we want to?
- Are there any current skills gaps in the organisation?
- How do we invest in the staff that we currently have?

Systems

- Do we have sufficient management control over our resources?
- Do we know what things cost?
- How do we make decisions?

Style

- What is our relationship to our users like?
- Do we present the kind of image that we want to?

Shared values

- Are the organisation's shared values clear?
- Is there a clear agreement about what is important?
- Is there a clear agreement about how we work?

Using the exercises

To get people to contribute to the plan needs some preparation. You need to be clear about the objective and purpose of each exercise and how the issues discussed can be carried forward into the planning process.

The following five points might be helpful to whoever is leading or facilitating any group planning session.

1 People need to feel safe.

   Participants to a good discussion need to understand why they are doing it. They also need to feel confident that the discussion will be properly led, that people will be listened to and that confidentiality will be respected. The group leader needs to ensure that the group has clear rules to operate to and should watch out for conflicts becoming personal.

2 Feelings are important.

   Many of the exercises are about making subjective judgements. Often people have a 'gut feeling' why something is a 'strength' or a 'weakness'. Hard facts are important, but there should be space in the process for people to express opinions and then work to a more objective position.

3 Often there is not one single correct answer.

   Understanding different perspectives is important. A treasurer might regard a project as a great success because it is fully funded, covers all of its costs and even brings in some money. Whereas a field worker might regard the same project as dull, lacking in direction and failing to deliver. The important issue is not getting to a single answer, but enabling both sides to see and understand the different perspectives. Once that has been achieved the organisation is more likely to be able to agree a shared strategy and plan.

4 Ensure that the discussion moves on.

The group leader needs to help the group move through a discussion. A useful process is to get everyone to work on the exercise individually or in pairs, then to share each analysis, identify points of consensus, discuss differing points, and then move on to identify options for future plans and development. The effective use of questions can guide the group from discussion to analysis to planning:

Discussion points: What do we have in common?

What different perspectives are there?

Analysis: What conclusions can we draw?

Why has this happened in this way?

What learning points can we draw for future actions?

Planning: What options are there for the future?

What kind of strategy is needed?

What would be the first steps in moving this forward?

5 Make sure the exercise is followed up.

The group leader has a key responsibility to ensure that the discussion is concluded and is followed up. The leader might choose to record the discussion by noting points of agreement and also points of disagreement. The leader should ensure that a process is agreed as to how the points from the discussion should be fed into the business planning process – for example by presenting options for change.

At what stage is your organisation's development?

How would you characterise your organisation's current stage of development?

> *Renewal*

What are the key organisational issues that it needs to tackle?

> - *Mgt Supervision*
> - *Volunteer Supervision*
> - *Volunteer feedback*
> - *Assessment of comm. Need*

Comparing mission and activity

This exercise aims to help your organisation compare its activities (services, programmes and projects) with its intended purpose and mission. For example, as part of their planning day, the Caldew neighbourhood project reviewed its six activities against its two main purposes of providing educational opportunities for those who have missed out and tackling poverty. This is what they came up with. Complete the exercise yourself to see whether the activites in which your organisation engages aligns with their stated purpose.

Activity	Our intended purpose	
	To provide educational opportunities for those that have missed out	To tackle poverty
Running an open to all computer room	Should be – but is it just a recreational space for young people?	Possibly – providing a resource for those excluded from technology. Needs refocusing.
Providing an outreach base for the College to run an adult education programme	Yes – but does it really bring in hard to reach groups?	Possibly in the longer term by helping people develop confidence and skills.
Running three healthy living groups	The sessions are targeted at hard to reach groups.	Proven link between poor health and poverty.
Running and supporting an adult literacy group	Yes.	Yes – overcomes a clear block to social inclusion.
Providing office space for councillors, the housing department and the Job Centre to run satellite sessions	Not sure? Are we just a convenient outpost?	Satellite sessions should increase people's access to service.
Providing meeting space and support for local clubs and societies.	Are they really part of our organisation?	Not sure.

In analysing the comparisons the following questions are useful:

■ How clear is our purpose or mission? Is it so vague that everything can be made to fit?

■ Is there a clear rationale as to why we run certain activities?

■ What are we driven by? A clear and compelling sense of purpose or just delivering things?

Misfits?

If there are activities or services that do not fit with the purpose it is useful to consider the following points.

Could it be that our stated purpose is out of date or no longer relevant to users?

Why are we doing this?

■ Is it a historical accident?

■ Have we just drifted into it?

■ Are we the best people to do it?

EXERCISE 10

Doing a SWOT analysis

Set out the strengths and weaknesses of your organisation as you see them. Note possible opportunities and threats which may emerge in the future.

Strengths	Weaknesses

Opportunities	Threats

EXERCISE 11

Looking outside – making comparisons

In the first column list all of the organisations that do similar work to yours. Then consider the similarities and differences between you and them. Then describe the current relationship and finally any ideas for how the relationship might develop.

Organisation to compare	Similarities to us	Differences to us	Current relationship	Strategic possibilities

EXERCISE 12

Predicting future trends and developments

	Next 12 months	1–3 years	Longer term
Available resources			
Changes in practice and how we work			
Changes in demand and needs			
Changes in the political or economic arena			
Changes in the environment and market			

EXERCISE 13

A portfolio matrix for your organisation

Question marks – new ideas, start-ups and pilots – innovative but not yet proven.

Stars – strong, dynamic and successful projects.

Cash cows – reliable and steady activities.

Dead dogs – activities that take up resources but produce little return or value.

Question marks	Stars

Cash cows	Dead dogs

What do you think of the balance of the portfolio?

What are the critical issues for each activity?

Sorting out the numbers

Some business plans consist of little more than financial projections. There has been a tendency, particularly from banks and some larger funding bodies, to ask that the business plan projects income for the next three years, gives a detailed cash-flow analysis and shows that the organisation is (and will remain in years to come) a safe and viable concern.

This is often a pointless exercise. Few organisations in any sector can accurately predict their financial position much beyond the next financial year.

However, a business plan needs to show the following.

- That the organisation is financially viable and that it has thought through its financial policy and likely income and expenditure in an intelligent and realistic way.
- That it has made sensible assumptions about its likely financial future.
- That it has realistically and fully costed its activities and taken into account the need for contingencies.
- That it has sufficient financial controls to manage and plan properly.
- That it has coherent financial management policies.

Increasingly investors are more interested in the assumptions behind a plan. This involves checking that the financial plan has been properly considered rather than checking every item of anticipated income and expenditure line by line.

This chapter looks at seven issues.

- Drawing up a model of how the organisation expects to operate.
- Forecasting income.
- Earning money from what you do (social enterprise).
- Establishing the break-even point and the break point.
- Establishing what an activity costs.
- Forecasting cash flow.
- Considering some key financial questions.

What financial information does the plan need?

As voluntary organisations grow and develop their financial processes and information needs to change. In the past all that really mattered was ensuring that sufficient funding was obtained to cover planned expenditure. The emphasis was on the bottom line. Today's tougher funding climate means that many organisations are facing difficult financial choices.

Contracts and service agreements require an organisation to cost and price individual projects and services accurately. In the past statutory bodies made a grant aid contribution to support an organisation. Contracting is about purchasing a specific service from an organisation at a predetermined price. If the price is wrong the service still has to be delivered.

Greater public scrutiny of voluntary organisations is expected. Voluntary organisations need to be open and transparent about how they use their funds and resources.

In putting together the business plan you need to give careful consideration as to how much financial information to include. How you present financial information will depend upon two factors.

1 How open you wish to be about your organisation's financial affairs. For example, some organisations negotiating contracts have felt in a weaker position because their potential purchasers have had full details of their financial arrangements.

2 Your ability to be accurate about future financial projections. The further you plan from the present, the less certain your financial projections will be. One organisation produced draft income and expenditure forecasts on the following basis.

Year one: Monthly projections.

Year two: Quarterly estimates.

Year three: A rough estimate of income and expenditure for the year.

How can you project income?

Many organisations are plagued by the short-term outlook of some funders. It is easy to get caught up in an April to April scramble for cash. An essential activity in a business plan is to try to predict income trends in future years.

The process of analysing income sources is often called a 'sensitivity analysis' in the jargon of business planning. This should consist of three elements.

1 Reviewing current position. How stable has the income been in the past?

2 How do we predict each source of income developing? What is likely to happen to it? What is it dependent on? How reliable will it be?

3 What action is needed to achieve the target? What can we do to secure this income? How can we protect or extend it through better marketing or better negotiating?

Possible income sources

- Grant aid from statutory bodies.
- Service agreements and contracts.
- Grants from trusts and companies.
- Public fundraising.
- Sponsorship.
- Legacies.
- Subscriptions and donations from members.
- Profit from trading operations.
- Earned income from the sale of services.
- Hire of resources.
- Investment income.
- Management fees.
- Consultancy fees.
- Income from users (such as rent).

CASE STUDY

Predicting trends in current income

A community arts agency produced the following prediction of its likely sources of income for the next three years.

Income source	Current position	Prediction of trend	Action needed
Council grant Leisure Committee	30% of income. Annually agreed. Use not specified.	Will evolve into service agreement. Will probably stay at same level plus inflation.	Push for three year agreement. Sort out negotiating strategy.
Regional Arts Board (RAB) funding	25% of income. Annually agreed.	Review by RAB to be carried out this year.	Follow up review. Monitor the changing funding criteria.
Commercial sponsorship for artist in residence	14% of income. Will end this year.	We could lose a management fee of £2,000.	Look for alternative sponsorship.
Fee earned for local estate work	12% of income from four contracts.	Difficult to predict. Do they cost more than we think?	Need to market outside current area.
Hire of building for events	9% of income.	Bookings down from previous years.	Need to review, market and develop pricing plan.
Office space rented to outside group	6% of income.	Not a realistic level.	Schedule rent review.
Donations Miscellaneous income	4% of income.	Will probably stay at this level with minimal effort.	Do we need to review our fundraising strategy?

This activity quickly identified some issues for the management to address:

- Does it really know what each activity costs?
- Did it properly cost out the full cost of a project or activity before taking it on?

One interesting aspect of this exercise was that no individual in the agency had responsibility for managing specific income. Hire of the building, office rent, donations and sponsorship were all organised on a very ad hoc basis. No one thought about them in a strategic way, but they accounted for 33 per cent of the agency's income.

Earning money from what you do

Over the past few years the move towards business planning and social or community enterprise has been one of the most talked about and talked up issues in the voluntary sector. Examples of charities earning money and visionary social entrepreneurs are held up as examples to follow. At its simplest social enterprise is about earning money from what an organisation does or from the expertise that it has.

It involves operating as a business, with services, products and customers, but with a social motive as the business should benefit the community. It can involve operating in two different, but overlapping worlds – a commercial one as well as a charitable one. However, voluntary organisations setting out to make money is not that new! Many organisations have traded or charged for their services. The movement around social enterprise has given it a much greater impetus and profile.

Social enterprise can take different formats including:

- creating a new organisation as a not for profit company;
- having separate trading structures within an organisation that work alongside the mainstream charitable activities;
- identifying and encouraging people to develop income generating opportunities in what you do already – for example, seeing an opportunity to charge some people for services.

Social enterprise can be an organisation or an activity. Examples of social enterprise include:

- direct trading ventures to the public or other 'businesses';
- operating shops, cafés, childcare and other ventures, but with the clear intent that profits are returned to benefit the charity;
- selling knowledge and expertise;
- charging for consultancy, training and publications to others;
- contracted services – gardening, environmental improvements and administrative support by bidding for contracts to take on specific activities.

CASE STUDY

A stalled plan

After Val's first month as director of the Meadow Centre three things were clear to her.

1. That there was very strong demand for the counselling and therapy services that the Centre offered.

2. That the Centre had a team of staff who were highly skilled and committed to the centre's vision of tackling stress in society.

3. That the Centre's income was too reliant on public sector grants and contracts.

Val spent time working on ideas to develop the Centre and came up with three ideas for generating income.

- Developing a sliding scale of charges for work with individuals seeking counselling. Val estimated that the majority of clients would still get a free service, but people who could afford it would be asked to contribute.

- The human resources director of a large local employer had expressed interest in the centre delivering an employee assistance service for their staff suffering from stress.

- The centre could develop a training programme in inter-personnel and communication skills.

Using her business experience Val drew up plans for each of these services and started to introduce the idea to key trustees and staff members. Val felt confident that these proposals would secure the Centre's work and take it onto a new level.

An away day was organised to work on the Centre's future strategy. The discussion that followed a Powerpoint presentation from Val was mainly negative. Members of staff were concerned that charging would take the centre away from its founding principles of reaching out to those most disadvantaged. Would those who pay get a better service – such as the offer of convenient appointment times? One worker suggested that he might as well go into or set up in private practice. The Centre's treasurer wondered if bringing in money would simply lead to their current statutory funders reducing their income.

(continued)

Talking over the session with the committee's Chair Val realised three things.

■ For it to work, any income venture had to fit in with the Centre's ethos and style.

■ That a trading venture had to be more than making money – she had not emphasised how the ideas could have extended the reach of the Centre, made it more independent and taken it into new areas of work.

■ She needed to demonstrate that by earning money the Centre would be able to create an income stream that it could use to work with the most disadvantaged clients, hard to reach groups or 'unpopular' causes that their current funders ignored. Trading could help the Centre meet its original mission.

There are several compelling reasons for developing income-generating schemes.

■ To create an unrestricted income stream – generating its own income can give an organisation an income that is not dependent on the changing policies of funders. Income from trading can give an organisation money that is not restricted or has to be used for a particular purpose.

■ To broaden the funding base – many voluntary organisations have seen social enterprise as a way of diversifying their funding and reducing their dependency on one or two main funders.

■ To develop the organisation – operating as a social business might raise management skills, improve marketing and build the organisation's profile.

■ As a way to meeting the mission – successful social enterprises can create jobs for clients and play a part in strengthening a local economy.

CASE STUDY

Recognising valuable skills

The manager of a medium-sized charity comments:

'It wasn't until we started thinking about social enterprise that we realised how much we gave away and also what valuable skills we had within our organisation.

In the past we shied away from asking to be paid properly for what we would do. A couple of years ago we developed a new and innovative way of working with our client group. After some good publicity, we started getting requests from people to visit us, or to see our materials or to speak at conferences. All we ever got in cash terms was travel expenses! We gave away our expertise. We could have packaged it up or even developed a franchise.

We are now developing training, publications and consultancy services. We now try to see our knowledge and expertise as a key asset.'

Getting started on social enterprise

As with any business idea, one of the first questions is to be clear that the organisation has or could have something of value that other people or organisations would be prepared to pay for. Often this comes from recognising the strengths of the organisation and being able to turn them into services or products. The business idea need not be a tangible product (selling products). It could equally be about the organisation's expertise or knowledge – its 'know how'.

It is important to spend time looking at the market that the enterprise will operate in. Finding out what other people do and comparing what else is on offer should lead to analysis of:

■ how the market works – how big is it and who buys and when?

■ who else is in the market – what is the nature of the competition?

The answers to these questions can help to define what the organisation intends to offer and also help to identify how it can best be marketed.

Does the organisation's constitution allow this kind of activity? In broad terms charity law allows trading if it advances the charity's primary purposes. The organisation's governing document needs to be examined and options such as creating a separate trading arm considered.

Does the organisation have the right kind of management, marketing and business skills? Can existing skills such as fundraising be developed into the skills involved in running a business?

Business models

In developing an idea for income generation or for a social enterprise it is useful to draw up a business case or a business model. A business model is a business plan for a project, idea or new venture that if agreed would be part of a bigger organisation. It should explain the idea, show the thinking behind it and demonstrate that it is feasible and viable.

Some business models are incredibly simple – 'the local authority gives us 90 per cent of the money, we scrape round for the rest… and then we spend it' – but as organisations grow and become more complex, understanding the model is important.

A business model shows how the business will work. It sets out how the organisation expects to develop, sell and distribute its services and also who and how it expects to buy them. It shows the key factors needed to make the business work. For example the business model for producing a quarterly magazine would need to show the relationship between circulation and advertising revenue (i.e. when circulation reaches a certain level, advertisers will probably pay more to advertise). Discussion of the business model can help to understand and test an idea. Analysis of a business model can focus on the following.

- Durability of the idea. Is there a sustainable business idea or is it based on an unproved market?
- The need to review assumptions. A social business might plan on the basis that it will still be based at the 'parent' charity's office and therefore enjoy cheap rent and the support of the charity's administration and office staff. If the business grows significantly is this a safe assumption?
- Risks. The model should identify the key business, financial and organisational risks involved.
- Full costing. Is the idea fully costed? How have overhead costs such as accommodation, management support been planned? Is there a danger that the main organisation will provide a 'hidden subsidy' to the trading venture?
- The possibility of speculation. A business model enables and encourages 'what if' questions such as what happens if business is much slower in the first year or what happens if particular costs rise. A good business model cannot accurately predict how the business will perform, but it does help to understand it and what needs to be done to achieve success.

Showing how it works – what's the business model?

All organisations are based on some kind of model or framework that shows how money can be raised or earned and then used to fund the organisation's work. Often the model is implicit or not described in any detail. In a business plan it is important that readers understand how the organisation intends to fund itself and the assumptions behind the overall financial framework.

In most voluntary organisations income is raised from donations, fees and payments for work done (contracts). This income is then used to fund the work. Increasingly organisations are developing more complex and creative models.

CASE STUDY

Different Business Models

A community arts centre developed a funding model based on three strands:

- Grants and service agreements from public authorities to pay the full cost of the centre's core programme of arts development work with young people. All funding would include an element to pay for the centre's running costs and core staff team.

- The centre would develop a programme of 'Arts in your life' services and products that it could market to schools, local agencies and companies. The programme would be costed to include a contribution to the centre's management cost.

- The centre would also offer for rent a set of rooms and run a cybercafé and a small-scale print shop. These activities would generate income to use to develop new projects.

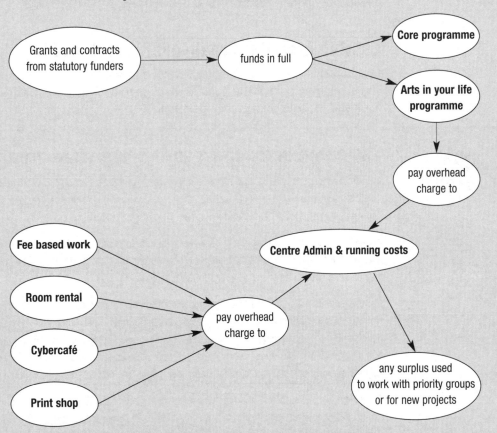

A counselling centre developed what it described as a cocktail of different forms of income to fund its work. The majority of its income was from a service agreement with a local authority. The centre had been able to develop other income streams such as charging some private clients, delivering an occupational health programme for a large employer and running a series of training courses in basic counselling skills. The centre's business plan set out the different funding and income streams, explained the relationship between them and how income from one area was intended to subsidise another.

Explaining the business model

A business model does three things.

- It sets out the assumptions behind the plan: the model shows the thinking behind how the organisation operates and shows how the organisation fits together.
- It shows the interdependency of different elements: the model sets out how different activities and different income streams relate to each other.
- It highlights potential risk: the model can show potential danger or exposure to risk. For example, the withdrawal of one relatively small funding source could have a serious impact throughout the system.

Developing trading or a social enterprise can have an impact on the internal management and style of the organisation. Any trading operation must fit with the purpose, values and identity of the organisation. A director of a charity that had encouraged income generation from trading commented on how 'two years in we have had to deal with an element of internal competition – one or two people seemed to believe that their work is more important because it brought money in – they expected a status and first call on things like admin support'.

The development of social enterprise within an organisation can have other benefits as well as bringing in money. It can bring in or develop a set of useful skills and processes such as market research, marketing, risk management and financial control and planning. It will ensure that management and business systems are sound. Another spin-off can be giving an organisation a renewed sense of its independence in that it is not totally dependant on the whims of one or two funders.

Establishing the break-even point and break point

In a profit-making venture the break-even point and the break point are of critical concern. The break-even point is the point at which income from trading starts to overtake the fixed and variable costs of the operation.

CASE STUDY

The community café's break-even and break points

A community café calculated that they would have to meet a fixed cost of £85 each week even if it sold no meals at all. The fixed costs would include rent, wages and payments on hire purchase (see the table below). The variable cost is £0.40 for every meal made. This is the additional cost of every meal sold at £0.75.

At 244 meals the café reaches the break-even point. Income from sales has overtaken the combined fixed and variable cost. At 244 meals the café moves into profit, the fixed cost remains the same and only the extra variable cost of each meal sold is added to the total cost.

However a point will be reached when the growth of the operation means that its ability to respond to growth is inadequate. At around 400 to 450 meals the café starts to hit break point. It needs to invest in more equipment, more space and more staff to cope with increased customer demand. If it fails to do this, it is likely that the service will start to suffer. The quality of both the food and the service will be reduced, staff could become stressed and customers might stop coming. The café could be harmed by its own success.

At, or even better well before, the break point, the café needs to have the cash to expand its capacity to do business. This will add to its fixed costs (taking them to £170 per week) and in the example shown takes the café (hopefully only temporarily) back into a loss. It could have planned for this by setting aside a certain sum each week to cover such expansion and increased cost.

Fixed costs: £85 per week
Variable costs: £0.40 (i.e. cost per meal)
Price: £0.75

Meals sold per week	Fixed cost £	Unit cost £	Total cost £	Income £	Profit/loss £
450	170	180	350	337.50	-12.50
400	85	160	245	300	55
350	85	140	225	262.50	37.50
250	85	100	185	187.50	2.50
244	85	97.60	182.60	183	0.40
200	85	80	165	150	-15
100	85	40	125	75	-50
0	85	0	85	0	-85

Break-even analysis has always had relevance when a service receives income for every time it gets used. For example, a hostel needs to fill so many beds each night to remain viable. For some, identifying the break-even and break point might not be so straightforward.

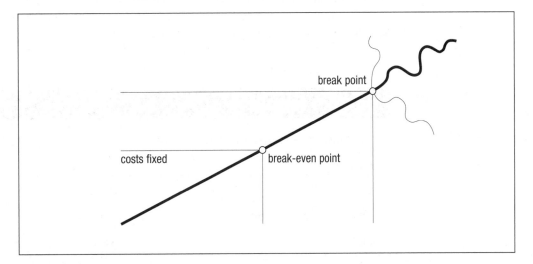

The break point is that point at which the service reaches capacity. New clients can only be dealt with if extra resources (human and physical) are provided. Every organisation has a point where it becomes viable and certainly a point at which if it continues to take on more work it will have gone past its capacity. Beyond the break point it will then start simply responding and crisis managing. It is worth noting that sometimes the most relevant break points are not to do with cash income. They could include staffing levels, casework systems and physical space.

Discussion of break-even and break points for voluntary organisations highlights several important strategic issues.

Many voluntary organisations have a culture that encourages people to go beyond the break point, never say 'no' and somehow manage to provide a service to more people with either the same or declining resources. The long-term consequence of this is that a service becomes led only by demand, it only reacts to pressure and sooner or later the quality of work suffers.

The problem of the break point is a problem of success. Demand for the service has outstripped the capacity to supply it. Several studies of small business failures point to growing too fast or growing beyond its capacity as reasons for failure. In many instances managing rapid growth and increasing demand is as hard as managing crisis and decline.

In a profit-making enterprise it should be possible to see the break point approaching, produce a business plan that shows the venture's success and gain the financial backing to obtain extra financial resources to take it over the break point. When a voluntary organisation reaches a break point it is highly unusual for a funding body to offer additional cash because the organisation is very busy. Several agreements between voluntary and statutory agencies are very clear about the minimum service requirements, but are silent about the point at which the service being purchased reaches break point and a further contract would have to be negotiated. Increasingly, strategic management is about identifying the current capacity of the organisation and managing demand in a fair and equitable way.

Establishing what an activity costs

Traditionally, budgeting in voluntary organisations has been about making sure that there will be sufficient income to meet projected expenditure. The focus has been on getting the 'bottom line' to balance. Changes in funding arrangements, the increased use of specific projects within organisations and an increased unwillingness to pay for core or administrative costs has led several agencies to move away from a traditional budget to one which more accurately shows the full cost of a specific activity.

Budget format

A traditional budget usually has the following format:

Income		Expenditure	
Council grant	......	Salaries	......
Trust and company donations	......	Administration	....
Fundraising	......	Building	.....
Sales income	......	Projects expenditure	.....
TOTAL		TOTAL	

The budget does not indicate what each activity or service costs. An alternative method of budgeting is called *cost centring* or *activity-based* budgeting. Several organisations are moving from a traditional budget to one in which all expenditure is charged to a particular activity or project.

A major development in this field is the emergence of Full Cost Recovery. The publication of the first edition of *Funding our Future* (2002) by the Association of Chief Executives of Voluntary Organisations (ACEVO) set out a model for organisations to use to fully cost their work. *Funding our Future*, now in its third edition, makes it clear that organisations could not simply hide away or ignore their core management and administrative costs. At the same time, the Government's Treasury's review *'The Role of the Voluntary and Community Sector in Service Delivery – A Cross Cutting Review'*, commented that:

> Funders should recognise that it is legitimate for providers to include the relevant elements of overheads in their cost estimates before providing a given service under service agreement or contract.

Central to cost centring is the division between direct and non-direct costs.

Direct costs are the costs that are only incurred as a direct result of running the particular activity. An organisation's decision to run education courses would involve the cost of trainers, room hire, course material and probably most of the education officer's time. If it did not run education courses it should not incur these costs.

Indirect costs are the shared organisational costs. They are costs that are difficult to apportion to a specific project or activity. Examples in the case study on page 58 'Working out the full costs' would be some of the manager's time, some administration costs and some building charges. Increasingly, organisations are finding it hard to obtain separate funding for indirect costs.

Moving to a cost-centred budget involves the following steps:

1 Identifying the cost centres to use. This could be related to income sources or to work functions such as particular projects, activities or geographic areas. The centres used should be clear and distinct areas.

2 Allocating expenditure that can be directly apportioned to each cost centre. This will include supplies, resources and people's time. This process could be done on the basis of past usage ('on average the rural project uses the minibus for a third of its available time'). The ACEVO model on Full Cost Recovery provides a useful template for this process.

3 Agreeing how the remaining expenditure (the things that cannot easily be allocated to a specific cost centre) should be dealt with. In the case study a fixed formula was used to divide the indirect costs between centres. The indirect cost is a charge to the activity or project to cover the central management or infrastructure costs.

Developing a cost-centred approach raises several issues.

Many voluntary organisations have been very poor at properly costing their work. The cost of spending or using other people's money can be high. Often the cost involved in operating and providing good management has not been properly identified, under costed or even ignored. This can easily lead to a long-term crisis of struggling to do 'quality work on the cheap'.

Several organisations who have moved into cost centres have realised that the real cost of an activity is often far more than the grant or contract income that they receive from a statutory authority. This can raise a policy issue: should a voluntary organisation subsidise work carried out for statutory bodies? It also may help negotiators adopt a more assertive approach in future contract discussions. There may be occasions when an organisation takes a strategic decision to take on an activity at below its full cost and either cross subsidise or fundraise to fill the gap. In the past, the lack of any real costing information has meant that organisations have often drifted into activities without any sense of the financial implications.

A negative side effect of cost centres is that it can create an unhelpful competitive tension within the organisation. People in one centre can start complaining that they 'are more profitable' than others. This needs careful management. Cost centres provide management information that can help with making priorities and attaching value to activities. The value of an activity will probably be measured in more than financial terms.

In some organisations the issue of what is a reasonable amount to spend on indirect costs as opposed to direct ones has become a controversial one. A hostel manager complained that she had to add on £62,000 to her annual costs to pay for her parent organisation. She doubted if she received anywhere near £62,000 worth of management and central services back in return. In other sectors the reduction of indirect central costs either through 'creative accounting' strategies or through 'downsizing' in which central services and jobs are cut has been pursued zealously. Perhaps a more useful approach is to look at how central services can 'add value' to the core projects and activities of the organisation through giving direction, providing support and the delivery of efficient services.

CASE STUDY

Working out the full costs

The community health team is a voluntary project set up to help people adopt a healthier lifestyle and increase well being. The team does this through information, providing advice and carrying out public campaigns.

The team currently has eight main activities:

- An education programme — Courses for teachers and health workers
- 'Good health' week — An annual health promotion week
- Rural project — Outreach work with isolated communities
- Resource centre — A library of materials for teachers to use
- HIV/AIDs Project — Awareness work on HIV/AIDs issues
- Youth Project — Work with 16–22 years old
- Public enquiries work — Telephone enquiry point
- Advocacy/development work — Support for local health partnerships and initiatives

Its current budget is:

Income	£
Contract from Primary Care Trust	117,000
Charitable trust grant for Youth Work	20,000
Project grant for work on HIV/AIDs	14,000
Income from courses	16,000
Income from sale and hire of resources	3,000
Council grant for Good Health Week	4,000
Total	**174,000**

Expenditure	£
Salaries	124,000
Admin costs	13,000
Resources	4,000
Minibus	3,000
Good Health	7,000
Telephone	6,000
Building costs	17,000
Total	**174,000**

The project's staffing is:

	£
Manager	28,000
Education Officer	23,000
Information Officer	22,000
Field Officer	22,000
Resources Officer	19,000
Admin worker (part time)	10,000
Total	**124,000**

The budget had existed in this format for several years. However, the Board decided to move to a different format that showed the full costs. Four reasons prompted this move.

- The budget did not show the full cost of individual activities or projects.
- Funders and purchasers wanted to know exactly what activities cost.
- The project needed better information for bids and contract negotiation.
- The project found it hard to raise money for core costs or policy work.

After some discussion the project agreed to divide the team's work into seven project or programme areas:

- Education work
- Resource Centre/Information work
- Youth Project
- HIV/AIDs work
- Rural project
- Good Health Week
- Policy development work

The first task was to divide all expenditure into three categories.

1 Direct project costs – expenditure directly linked to delivering services.

2 Project support costs – costs incurred in supporting the delivery of services.

3 Overhead costs – central functions (administration, finance and personnel) plus the cost of governing the organisation and of organisational development.

The first step was for each staff member to divide their time up. Using an activity log team members allocated their time as follows:

	Manager	Education Officer	Information Officer	Field Officer	Resources Officer	Admin Worker	Total
Education							
>direct	5%=£1,400	70%=£16,100			10%=£1,900		19,400
>support	5%=£1,400					10%=£1,000	2,400
Resource/Info							
>direct	5%=£1,400	15%=£3,450	70%=£15,400	5%=£1,100	80%=£15,200		36,550
>support						20%=£2000	2,000
Youth Project							
>direct				20%=£4,400			4,400
>support	5%=£1,400					5%=£500	1,900
HIV/AIDs							
>direct	15%=£4,200	10%=£2,300	10%=£2,200	5%=£1,100			9,800
>support	5%=£1,400				5%=£950	5%=£500	2,850
Rural Project							
>direct	5%=£1,400		10%=£2,200	60%=£13,200			16,800
>support	5%=£1,400					5%=£500	1,900
Good Health							
>direct	5%=£1,400	5%=£1,150	5%=£1,100	10%=£2,200			5,850
>support	5%=£1,400					5%=£500	1,900
Policy							
>direct	20%=£5,600		5%=£1,100				6,700
>support						5%=£500	500
Overheads	20%=£5,600				5%=£950	45%=£4,500	11,050
Total	28,000	23,000	22,000	22,000	19,000	10,000	124,000

The next stage was to allocate the non-salary costs.

	Admin	Resources	Minibus	Good health	Phones	Building costs
	13,000	4,000	3,000	7,000	6,000	17,000
Education	1,500		150			3,000 _4650_
Resource/Info	2,000	3,400	200		2,500	4,000
Youth project	500	300	800			3,000
HIV/AIDs	500	200	50			2,000
Rural project	600		750			2,000
Good health	500	100	200	7,000		400
Policy	400		50			2,000
Overheads	7,000		800		3,500	600
	13,000	4,000	3,000	7,000	6,000	17,000 _50,000_

The final allocation:

	Direct staff costs	Project support	Non-salary direct costs	Total
Education	19,400	2,400	4,650	26,450
Resource/Info	36,550	2,000	12,100	50,650
Youth project	4,400	1,900	4,600	10,900
HIV/AIDs	9,800	2,500	2,750	15,050
Rural project	16,800	1,900	3,350	22,050
Good health	5,850	1,900	8,200	15,950
Policy	6,700	500	2,450	9,650
Overheads	11,050		11,900	22,950

The final stage is to share the total overhead cost out amongst the seven projects. The Board decided that the simplest way to do this was to divide the £22,950 evenly amongst them.

Forecasting cash flow

Business planners are often inclined to be very enthusiastic about cash-flow forecasts as many organisations have learnt a hard lesson that an anticipated cash surplus can easily be blown away by budgeted income not arriving on time. Cash-flow forecasting is about ensuring that there will always be sufficient cash available to meet anticipated expenditure.

In reality it is very difficult to predict accurately exact income and expenditure patterns and cash inflows and outflows for more than eighteen months ahead. However, a business plan needs to show the following.

- That the impact of cash flow has been considered.
- That cash flow will be managed.
- That the organisation will have sufficient cash reserves to meet its needs.
- That the organisation understands its patterns of cash flow including seasonal ups and downs.

In looking at a cash-flow forecast it is useful to consider the following questions.

1 Are there any points at which we will not have sufficient cash to meet our outgoings?
2 What is our minimum monthly operating cost?
3 How much working capital do we need to pay for expansion and development?
4 What could we quickly do to improve our cash flow position in an emergency?

Managing cash flow

A business plan may indicate the steps taken to manage and improve cash flow.

Tactics for managing cash flow might include:

- writing payment schedules (possibly with penalty clauses) into contracts;
- monitoring payment of fees and grants;
- tighter control of people who owe you money;
- faster invoicing;
- spreading out expenditure in instalments;
- delaying some expenditure;
- delaying payment of certain bills;
- better banking arrangements.

Key financial questions to consider

The following ten strategic financial questions are useful in appraising an organisation's financial arrangements and financial strategy as part of the business planning process:

Do we have sufficient working capital?

Working capital is calculated by subtracting current liabilities from current assets. On a balance sheet, this is usually called net current assets. Every organisation needs sufficient working capital to ensure that cash flow can be managed, to develop new projects and to cope with unexpected events. Several voluntary organisations live on a hand to mouth existence where the slightest financial problem can cause problems. Many organisations have not been able to follow up opportunities due to a lack of working capital.

Do we know what it costs to operate?

Increasingly, organisations are having to develop accurate costing systems that identify the true cost of a specific activity or service. Costing needs to be accurate and realistic. It should fully take into account both direct and indirect costs and provide regular information that will ensure proper cost control.

CASE STUDY

Drawing up a cash-flow projection

opening cash balance:

	12 months	April	May	June	July	August	September	October	November	December	January	February	March
opening cash balance:		500	21,130	14,920	14,740	7,640	1,190	-980	14,300	11,180	5,160	3,690	1,420

Income	12 months	April	May	June	July	August	September	October	November	December	January	February	March
Council grant	30,000	15,000						15,000					
Arts Board	25,000	10,000						10,000			5,000		
Sponsorship	14,000			6,000					4,000			4,000	
Fee Income	12,000	2,000					5,000			1,000			4,000
Building hire	9,000	900	700	500	300	100	300	500	1,000	1,700	1,400	800	800
Rent income	6,000	500	500	500	500	500	500	500	500	500	500	500	500
Donations/Misc	4,000	400	350	350	250	250	300	400	350	350	300	350	350
TOTAL INCOME	100,000												
monthly income:		28,800	1,550	7,350	1,050	850	6,100	26,400	5,850	3,550	7,200	5,650	5,650

Expenditure	12 months	April	May	June	July	August	September	October	November	December	January	February	March
Salaries	42,500	3,220	3,260	3,330	3,500	3,500	3,670	3,670	3,670	3,670	3,670	3,670	3,670
Building cost	13,000	1,100	1,000	1,200	1,000	1,000	1,000	1,000	1,600	1,100	1,000	1,000	1,000
Admin	18,750	2,000	1,600	1,500	1,500	1,400	1,500	1,500	1,600	1,600	1,550	2,000	1,000
Phones	3,000	750			750			750			750		
Festival	7,200			600	200	500	1,200	3,000	700	800	100	100	
Projects	7,750	700	1,300	500	800	300	500	500	500	800	1,000	350	500
Equipment	8,000	400	600	400	400	600	400	700	900	1,600	600	800	600
TOTAL EXPENDITURE	100,200												
monthly expenditure:		8,170	7,760	7,530	8,150	7,300	8,270	11,120	8,970	9,570	8,670	7,920	6,770
closing cash balance		21,130	14,920	14,740	7,640	1,190	-980	14,300	11,180	5,160	3,690	1,420	300

(opening balance + monthly income − monthly expenditure)

CASE STUDY

A tale of two cultures

In the space of two weeks, the director of a community project had two different discussions about her agency's financial policy

The voluntary sector liaison officer at the local authority told her that 'concern was being expressed' within the authority that the project's recently published annual report had shown an 'operating surplus' of £7,000. The project had decided to build up a reserve fund equivalent to six weeks operating costs to cover cash flow, develop new ideas and cover any contingency. The local authority took a dim view of this. Council money was supposed to be spent on local needs, not sit in a bank account. The possibility of 'clawing back' unspent money was mentioned.

A week later a manager from a potential corporate sponsor visited to assess a proposal the project had made. The manager concluded the review by drawing attention to the lack of any forward financial strategy and that a 'well managed organisation should be building up a significant reserve fund for longer term investment'.

This case raises three issues.

- The need to educate some funders and purchasers about the importance of sensible financial management practice. The business plan can play a useful role in this – it can set out the need for a sensible contingency fund and explain how any reserves are earmarked for a specific purpose.
- The importance of managing the relationship with funders. City corporations spend heavily on 'investor relations' – a form of internal marketing to stakeholders. Could a marketing strategy avoid such frustrations?
- A business plan should set out and make the case for a sound financial policy. If an organisation has developed reasonable reserves it needs to explain the reasons for them in a positive and not defensive way in the plan.

How do we price our work?

The cost of an activity should be based on rational facts. The price that a service is offered at is usually based on a tactical or marketing decision. Three possible strategies for pricing work are available:

a *Plus cost.* The cost is 'marked up' by a fixed percentage to create some surplus and possibly also to allow some room for negotiation with purchasers.

b *Under cost.* The fee agreed is below the actual cost. The organisation takes on a piece of work in the full knowledge that it will need to subsidise it. Possible reasons include: to attract future work; because the organisation's cash-flow demands cash at any cost; or because the organisation is so committed to the activity that it is prepared to invest its own money in it. There may be occasions when an organisation does take on work under cost, but it needs to have very clear reasons for doing so.

c *The price is set by the market.* There is a 'going rate' or an agreed rate for the activity set by the purchaser or by other organisations. The organisation needs to see if it can recover its costs (or even create a surplus) within the price that has already been set.

Can we control the patterns of cash flow?

Managing cash flow is important. Ensuring that future funding arrangements take cash flow into account, scheduling income and expenditure and agreeing payment schedules can all help to overcome potential cash-flow problems.

How much does it cost to use other people's money?

The resistance of some funders to contribute to indirect costs or overheads has meant that the true cost of operating has sometimes been ignored. Some organisations have taken on projects where the income only meets the direct costs. The cost of having the project in the organisation is ignored.

Is the balance between direct and indirect costs right?

Getting the right balance between project costs and organisational costs can be hard. Some organisations suffer from having an over-staffed and over-resourced centre and an under-resourced front line. What is a reasonable balance between the centre and the projects? Is the centre too large for the current level of project activity? Does it add value to the project work?

Are we managing our income as well as our expenditure?

Most organisations have controls over their expenditure that stop them going over budget. Is income also managed? Is sufficient attention paid to ensuring that income keeps to target, that shortfalls are picked up early, and that the future sources of income are carefully researched and managed? Is there any potential to charge for our services or to move into trading.

What sort of contingency fund do we need?

A contingency fund is an essential part of good financial arrangement. Contingency funds cover unexpected cash-flow problems and unforeseen events and circumstances. There has sometimes been resistance to building one up.

How will we replace capital items that depreciate over time?

Most capital items lose value over time. Each year the vehicles or equipment that the organisation owns reduce in value. On a balance sheet this is known as depreciation. The rate of depreciation depends on how long the item is expected to last, a proportion is written off every year and some funds should be allocated to a fund to replace the asset at the end of its useful life. It is useful to check that there is sufficient money in the replacement fund to meet likely replacement costs and that the depreciation timetable is accurate. One computer training centre found out that their accountant had assumed that their computers would be replaced every ten years, when it was likely that they would last for three years at the very most. Money needs also to be set aside for repairs, refurbishment and decoration.

Do we have sufficient financial skills?

Do the in-house financial people (e.g. treasurer, finance officer) have full control and are they able to provide regular and accurate monitoring information? Are the external financial advisers (e.g. accountant or auditor) useful in financial planning and aware of tax, VAT and investment issues?

Ten costs often ignored

The following ten costs are ones which are often underestimated or simply ignored.

Start-up costs

One off costs involved with launching or establishing a project. Staff recruitment costs, moving in costs and launch publicity costs are often underestimated or create an early cash-flow problem.

Slow-start costs

Sometimes services start slower than anticipated. Organisations that sell their services or receive unit contracts can experience below target performance at what can often be an expensive time due to extra costs involved in the service's start-up.

Marketing costs

Publicity costs, communication and image building costs are often ignored leading to poor or amateurish public relations that can cause credibility problems.

Working capital

Working capital is money which is not allocated or dedicated. It allows you to develop new projects and experiment. A lack of working capital means that new ideas and opportunities have to be ignored.

Research and development costs

Costs involved in user consultation, needs identification and service evaluation are often expensive and should be built into service budgets and plans to demonstrate good management practice.

Cash-flow costs

Many organisations operate to very tight cash-flow plans. A delayed payment from a funder or unanticipated expense can easily knock a budget off course. Anticipating cash-flow problems and making necessary arrangements to survive a cash shortage can lead to extra costs.

Management and administrative costs

An extra project will usually demand extra management and administrative time and space from the main organisation. There is a danger of simply adding projects and activities on until the systems break down. Extra administration time, payroll costs, computer usage and management time all need to be calculated. Volunteer management is another related cost.

Replacement and repair costs

Capital items will usually need to be replaced at some stage. Items such as computers, office equipment and other resources will need replacing at some stage. Many organisations have a replacement fund which accumulates cash for such costs. Is the contribution to the replacement fund sufficient?

Contingency costs

Staff maternity leave, sickness cover, legal costs and emergency repairs are all examples of contingency costs. Some organisations now hold a central contingency fund to which all projects contribute. Some contingency costs can be met by insurance cover.

Close-down costs

There will often be costs involved in closing down a fixed-term project that need to be built in. These could include evaluation costs, accounting charges, repairs and replacement costs of loaned equipment and buildings and staff costs.

EXERCISE 14

A trading venture checklist

This list is a starting point for checking that the ideas behind a trading venture have been fully worked out.

Strategic issues

1 Is the venture in line with our overall purpose and values? ☐

2 Does it fit with our organisation's strategy? ☐

3 What reaction might we get from users or funders? ☐

Business issues

4 Has the intended service or product been clearly defined? ☐

5 Have the legal and tax issues been properly considered? ☐

6 Has it been fully costed? ☐

7 What is the likely pattern of cash flow? ☐

8 How would start-up or slow-start costs be met? ☐

9 Are the potential risks involved reasonable? ☐

Organisational

10 Do we have the skills, systems and time for this venture? ☐

11 Are we sure that this venture will complement our main work? ☐

12 Is the level of organisational input into the venture worthwhile? ☐

The checklist is not designed to determine whether or not to go ahead with a venture. Its purpose is to ensure that the key issues have been properly worked out and to identify areas for further consideration.

Predicting trends in current income

In column A, list all your current sources of income. In column B, note the proportion of your income this particular source currently represents. Also note any other relevant details for example, if the income is scheduled to end. In column C, describe what you currently know or predict is likely to happen to this income source (e.g. will it get bigger or smaller or will the availability of it change?). In column D, note any action that you need to take to secure or better manage this income source.

A. Income source	B. Current position	C. Prediction of trends	D. Action needed

EXERCISE
16

A financial health check

This exercise aims to help the planning process by focussing on three issues:

1 The recent financial management and performance of the organisation.

2 The importance of developing a coherent financial policy for the organisation.

3 The need to think about finance in a strategic way and not simply a bureaucratic way.

Think about the past few years and future possibilities and answer the following questions.

Financial history

How effective has the organisation been at costing projects? Have budgets usually been accurate or have certain costs been ignored or badly estimated?

What has been the pattern of cash flow in the organisation? Have there been any regular peaks and troughs?

How have been costs allocated in the organisation? Have the core costs (i.e. management charges, administrative overheads) been properly recognised and reasonably shared out?

What has the balance sheet looked like? What has been the liquidity ratio, i.e. how much cash (current assets) has been available to pay off current liabilities?

EXERCISE 16 continued

Financial management and systems

Have there usually been adequate systems of financial control within the organisation?

Do budget holders receive information which is up-to-date, relevant and accurately monitors planned income and expenditure in relation to actual performance?

Does the organisation's financial system give accurate information on what specific services and projects cost (including their contribution to the organisation's indirect costs)?

Are any particular costs volatile or highly variable? How will this effect the business plan? Can they be controlled better?

Financial management and systems (continued)

Are there sufficient financial skills within the organisation to:

control income and expenditure:

accurately cost projects:

develop and project financial plans:

Do you anticipate any modifications to your budgeting or accounting systems?
What improvements are needed?

Financial policy

Is sufficient income set aside for reserves and contingency?

What proportion of the organisation's turnover would be reasonable to carry as a reserve or contingency fund?

Is sufficient income set aside to cover depreciation and for replacement costs?

Are the full costs of operating services and projects known?

Is the balance between central charges and direct project costs fair?

EXERCISE 16 continued

Financial projections

Over the next two years can you predict how income sources will develop?

which income sources do you predict will increase:	which income sources do you predict will decline:

What are your minimum operating costs in a month?

How flexible is your income? What proportion of your income is:

'earmarked' or committed for a particular expenditure i.e. its use is restricted:	dedicated from one year to another (for example salaries for permanent staff, contractual obligations to suppliers):	Is there sufficient flexibility available to the organisation about how it uses its income?

Does current spending accurately reflect current priorities?

What costs could be reduced:

direct project costs:	indirect organisational overheads:

Financial strategies

Can you anticipate any significant changes in your organisational cost base over the next few years?

How effective is your charging or pricing policy?

Is there a coherent policy behind the charges that you make for your services to statutory purchasers, funders and consumers?

what sort of pricing strategy do you currently use:

how does this compare to other organisations doing similar work:

how might this change:

EXERCISE
16
continued

Identifying a financial strategy

After reviewing your answers to the previous questions try to answer the following points:

what financial choices does the organisation have:

if the organisation were starting again what would be different about how it organised its finances:

what are the financial priorities for the organisation:

Setting the strategic direction

After clarifying what the organisation is for, taking stock of its development to date and obtaining a clearer financial picture, the planning process can now move onto setting a strategic direction.

Different definitions of strategy exist. In most definitions of organisational strategy the following elements are present.

- Making decisions about priorities.
- Linking current activities to future plans.
- Setting a direction or route for the organisation.
- Obtaining resources for the new direction.
- Managing change and setting objectives.

Most organisations (public, private or voluntary) were designed to allow vertical systems of command and control. People at the top of the organisation make important decisions and plans are transmitted down the organisation by managers and supervisors to the people who are responsible for carrying them out.

In many organisations these levels do not link together at all well. Policymakers (senior managers and committee members) churn out policy papers, develop plans and demand change. People working at the operations level feel frustrated that new initiatives from the top and 'change for change's sake' get in the way of the real work of the organisation. Any sense of strategy that links policy to the day-to-day work is missing.

Other criticisms of this structure are that it mitigates against teamwork, slows down communication (as the structure gets bigger) and prevents senior managers from seeing the impact of their work. Effective business planning and strategic management requires good internal communication, good feedback and an ability to think about the whole of the organisation and not just specific departments.

Often strategic management is about deciding what not to do as much as what to do. A key, and often difficult, challenge is being able to say no to activities and projects that although potentially valuable could overstretch the organisation.

This chapter will look at four issues.

1 Establishing the assumptions behind the plan.
2 Identification of the organisation's limits.
3 Identifying strategic choices.
4 Agreeing and setting a strategic direction.

Establishing the assumptions behind the plan

Any planning process involves making some assumptions upon which planning can be based. Some commercial planners develop complex future-based scenarios to test out future possibilities. Other people rely on intelligent and informed guesswork. A business plan should set out its central assumptions, as readers might wish to know the assumptions upon which the rest of the plan is based.

One approach is to list key assumptions under a series of headings:

Assumptions	Examples of assumptions made
Demand and needs	'That referrals will stay at the same rate over the next two years.'
	'That demand for respite care will continue to rise.'
External developments	'That the local authorities will increasingly move towards spot or user based contracts.'
	'That other agencies who work in this field will continue to charge a similar fee to ours.'
Internal developments	That we will still be able to recruit support and retain a volunteer team at its current level.'
	'That staff turnover will remain at its current level.'
Financial	'That for the next two years increases in fee rates will meet inflation and pay awards.'
	'That our fundraising income will rise by five per cent each year for the next three years.'

Assumptions need to be credible, discussed openly and periodically checked. The danger of operating where an assumption no longer applies is common place. It is useful to look for factors that might contradict or challenge the assumption and to test out how safe the assumption is. It is worthwhile to consider what the organisation would need to do if the assumption did not play out.

CASE STUDY

A limit on strategy

The 'honeymoon period' in Kerry's new job as development manager for a charity for people with learning difficulties did not last long. She had been employed to research, design and set up new projects and initiatives. The charity desperately needed to improve its services and develop a commitment to user involvement. In her first few months, she developed proposals for three small projects. At first the reaction of her colleagues was very supportive.

Every six months managers met together for a planning day. The bulk of Kerry's first meeting was given over to consideration of her proposals. None of the managers present disagreed in principle with the proposals. However, each proposal was subject to detailed examination of the potential risk, the financial implications and the other costs. Kerry agreed to produce further reports and feasibility studies.

Three months later all the projects were starting to 'slide off the drawing board'. However much extra information she produced, the projects were still being deferred.

Kerry fully understood that all new proposals needed rigorous review. However, she felt frustrated that many of the charity's current services were poor or in decline, but were never subject to any kind of review at all. Some were even at odds with the charity's recent statement of values and vision. Once projects had been established and were up and running they carried on being allocated resources every year regardless. It was as if strategic management only applied to the consideration of new things and not to looking at current activities.

Identification of the organisation's limits

All organisations have limits. Discussion of organisational strategy without reference to the organisation's limits is pointless day dreaming. Different sorts of limits exist. Some are fixed and some are more negotiable.

Possible limits include the following.

Physical

'Our current office could only cope with one more member of staff.'

Legal and constitutional

'Moving into this area of work could take us beyond our legal powers as a charity.'

Level of manageable risk

'To run this number of innovative and pioneering projects would be unacceptable to our trustees.'

Human

'Our current staff team are not skilled in this area of work.'

Resource

'To develop in such a way would stretch our management and communication systems.'

Financial

'To continue with this kind of funding would seriously harm our cash flow.'

Usually the most obvious limits are the resource or financial ones. However, it is interesting to look at how an organisation's traditions, practices and long-term commitments can also be a limiting factor.

Three questions are useful in reviewing the limiting factors.

1 How fixed is each limiting factor?

2 What creates the limiting factor?

3 What would we have to do to change it?

A useful exercise is to consider how the organisation would be different if it were to be created today. What would the organisation look like? What services would be provided? What would be the relationship to service users? It is interesting that many limiting factors are the direct product of the organisation's history. Some organisations have adopted a technique called zero base budgeting. Managers rebuild the budget for each activity as if they were starting it again. The case for expenditure and staff time has to be justified against the organisation's strategy. It is interesting as a result of this exercise how many limiting factors are challenged as resources previously committed are redirected to other priorities.

Same mission – different strategies

In 1986, health workers, community activists and people infected by HIV came together in a Midlands town to create an organisation to 'do something about AIDs'. After a year of hard work raising the issue, running HIV awareness courses and providing practical support to people with HIV, the group held an away-day to review progress. A key outcome of the day was a mission:

'To support people infected and affected by the disease and to overcome the ignorance and prejudice that surrounds it.'

The organisation's history could be described in three phases.

1   Early days: driven by a feeling of impending crisis. Volunteer led. Fast growth. Self help.

2   Early to late 1990s: appointment of staff to deliver a range of personal care, support and advocacy services to service users, development of a training programme delivered to key groups and communities.

3   New phase: strong sense of change caused by the development of drug regimes that kept infected people alive, a reduced public profile about the disease and changes in funding practices. A new direction was agreed that would focus much more on helping people to live with the disease, provide information about drug treatment and also take education and prevention work into the mainstream.

At their most recent away-day, one of the original founding members commented that the original mission was still relevant, but that the organisation's strategy for delivering it had had to change and respond to the needs, demands and opportunities that existed.

This case shows how an organisation's mission should give it a longer-term sense of purpose and also how good strategy needs to be driven by being in touch with external developments and change.

Identifying strategic choices

All organisations have choices available to them. Doing nothing is one choice. Identifying choices and options for the future should be a participatory process that involves all individuals.

A useful approach is to start by posing options for the future. Possible options might include:

- Should we grow, stay the same or get smaller?
- What aspects of our work should we do more of or less of?
- What geographic areas should we do more in or less in?
- What style of work should we do more of or less of?
- Which client groups should we target?
- Should we become more specialist or more generalist?
- What alliances or relationships with others should we develop?

At this stage it is useful to bring into the discussion the users' perspective and the organisation's mission. The focus of the direction needs to be on what the outside world needs and not just what feels comfortable for people in the organisation.

The list of options probably will be more than the organisation can deal with, so some sort of clear criteria are needed to evaluate possible choices. One agency worked through the following four points in relation to each option that emerged:

1   What is (or should be) distinctive about us as an organisation? Does this
    strategic option fit with our core mission and values?

2   What are we effective at? What works? What do we do consistently well? Is our expertise
    best suited to this option?

3 What are our priorities? What needs are most important to meet? Does this option fit with our priorities?

4 Will this option be financially viable or if not is it important enough to subsidise it? Will we be able to deliver?

Each option was applied to the above criteria and graded accordingly. A number were quickly rejected, others were combined together and five were picked as the main driving force of the organisation.

CASE STUDY

Identifying options by using scenarios

The Community Arts Team had reached a critical point in the agreement of its future strategy. In the ten years since it had been set up it had developed a track record of running successful projects and programmes. Often the initiative or idea had come from spotting a pot of money and developing a project to fit with it. The team decided it needed a strategic plan to guide its future development.

Working with a consultant the team analysed its development to date. It reviewed past projects, looked at what other agencies were doing and identified key external trends and opportunities. The team soon realised that it had far too many ideas as to how it could develop than it could possibly manage or resource. To move the plan forward the team developed a list of possible options and choices as to how the team could develop over the next three to five years.

Scenario 1: Aim to stay roughly as we are.

This option assumed that the team would continue to be able to obtain funding and support to carry on with the same pattern of activities and projects.

Scenario 2: Focus on community regeneration.

The team operated in an area scheduled for a major investment of government regeneration funds. This scenario would involve the team in working with the newly created regeneration partnership and using art forms to involve local people, encourage feedback and also to improve the urban environment.

Scenario 3: Become a community business.

The team could develop a number of small to medium-scale social businesses such as an internet café, an arts venue and an education and training programme that could operate on a proper business basis. Any profit made would be used to subsidise other activities.

Scenario 4: Reduce our focus.

This option would mean that the team would only work with young people.

This focus would give greater cohesion to the team and was based on a recognition that the team's greatest skills and competency were in working with younger people.

Scenario 5: Link up with a partner.

The final option recognised that the team had developed a strong working link with a local theatre company. In many respects there were strong overlaps between their work. This option would involve much more shared working, joint bidding to run projects together and sharing of some resources. A longer-term possibility of merger would be explored.

The team presented each of the options to a special meeting of their Management Board. Each scenario was evaluated against the team's mission and the Board's assessment of local need and possible funding. For some scenarios the Board was able to do a simple cost/benefit analysis setting out possible pros and cons. Careful facilitation led the Board away from trying to do all of them to a position where a number of elements from three scenarios were combined.

Participants felt that the process worked. Staff and Board members felt positive that there was not just one possible way forward presented. The discussion on possible scenarios had to be informed by an understanding of the changing environment that the agency operated in.

Agreeing and setting a strategic direction

Agreeing a strategic direction and aims involves constant reference back to the limiting factors and the overall mission. The process involves a continual movement between generating options, making priorities and working within the limiting factors.

At each stage the language of the plan changes. The mission statement will be hard to measure and act on. It is a statement of intent, not of specific action. The strategic aims need to indicate the clear direction and priority of the organisation for its immediate future. The objectives should be task-centred and provide a measurable work plan for the organisation.

Experience in several organisations is that anything more than six to seven strategic aims leads to a plan (and an organisation) that is fragmented, confused and pulling in different directions.

Strategic aims need to:

- indicate a clear direction;
- be focused on intended outcomes;
- be integrated with other aims;
- be realistic and attainable.

Determining a future strategy often involves difficult decisions. Turning down someone's favourite project, deciding to withdraw from an area of work or shifting resources from one area to another will usually involve anxiety and conflict. As much attention will have to be paid to what the organisation is not going to do as to what it is.

CASE STUDY

Moving from mission through strategy to objectives

The Eastside business advice agency was set up to help inner city residents explore the possibility of becoming self-employed and creating small businesses. It is strongly committed to equal opportunities and full access to its services.

The agency's mission is:

'The agency exists to support a viable and sustainable local economy. To provide high quality advice training and support to emerging or newly created small businesses. In carrying out this mission it will ensure that highest standards of quality assurance and equal opportunities apply throughout.'

Strategic aims

The agency agreed four strategic aims to guide all of its work over the next two years.

1 To continue to provide affordable and effective advice, counselling and information services to new or potential businesses.

2 To provide a high quality training programme for business owners in three areas: management skills, marketing and quality assurance.

3 To support cooperation between new businesses, encourage marketing of inner city businesses and identify new business opportunities.

4 To investigate and pilot ways of supporting businesses facing insolvency.

Specific objectives

For aim 3, 'To support cooperation between new businesses, encourage marketing of inner city businesses and identify new business opportunities' there are six objectives.

1 To encourage three inner city business networks through monthly breakfast seminars and quarterly business fora. The fora should aim to attract 150 participants in total (100 hours).

2 To organise four self-financing business advertisement campaigns promoting local business (30 hours).

3 To create a woman's business forum that will have a minimum of 20 participants and be able to be self managing (60 hours to be implemented by February).

4 To organise an inner city business exhibition target attendance 400 people (300 hours, planned date in October, budget: £12,000).

5 To have developed and implemented a strategy to raise funds for a food purchasing and distribution cooperative (75 hours first report to January management committee).

6 To participate in the management committee of the electronic village steering group (45 hours).

The objectives were produced by the relevant team member. They estimated how much time they would spend on each item as an indicator of priorities. The objectives became the work plan for each staff member.

Writing strategies

A template for writing strategies is set out in Exercise 21, page 87. The template can form the basis of the plan and also lead onto individual and operational work planning.

There is a danger that senior managers will write too much of the plan. Clearly trustees and managers have the responsibility for the mission and agreeing the strategic aims, but if they involve themselves in the detail of the operational objectives then the plan will never properly become the property of the organisation. One agency adopted a four-stage approach to agreeing its strategy.

First a joint staff and management committee meeting agreed a mission statement. After considerable discussion the management committee agreed five aims. Each aim was then delegated to an appropriate staff group who reviewed their activities and worked out a detailed work plan within the boundary set by the core aims. The management committee then agreed all the work objectives.

CASE STUDY

Appraising new projects

At their annual planning day the management committee and staff of a community development agency discussed four new initiatives or ideas that the agency could become involved in. The four ideas were tested against six criteria.

- Does it fit with our stated mission and core values?
- Is there a definite need for it?
- Does it fit with our strategy?
- Is it sustainable? – does it have a long-term future?
- Do we have the capacity to run it – skills, expertise, physical space?
- Will the project's direct and indirect costs be covered – will it be funded on a full cost recovery basis?

Criteria	Possible new idea			
	Working with the local crime prevention partnership	Setting up a food co-operative selling healthy foods	Opening up an internet café	Helping to set up a local credit union
Fits with our mission and values?	Yes – provided it genuinely involves local people.	Yes – fits with combating poverty and improving health.	Yes – supporting access to education.	Yes – fits with combatting poverty.
Is there a definite need for it?	Community survey shows that fear of crime is growing.	A core group of local volunteers are interested.	Not sure! Is there a real and proven need?	Yes – advice centre reports an upward trend in debt.
Does it fit with our strategy?	This would be a new area for us and would be (yet another) strategic priority.	Yes – supporting locally ran initiatives is a key priority.	Hard to see how it fits into our current priorities.	Yes - supporting locally run initiatives is a key priority.
Is it sustainable?	Don't know – funding for the partnership has only been agreed for the next year.	If successful – could develop into a social business with a declining need for external funding.	Prospect of initial funding – no guarantee of revenue support and replacement costs.	Experience elsewhere suggests that if it builds up sufficient members it could be viable in 3 to 5 years.
Do we have the capacity to run it?	Would take up staff time.	Yes – we have successfully supported similar initiatives.	Would mean reorganising office space.	Yes – initially we could house it and offer support.
Will the project's direct and indirect costs be covered?	Our staff time involved in participating in the partnership is unlikely to be reimbursed.	Yes – it would be fully costed and treated as a separate cost centre.	Not sure.	Yes.

Ten ways in which funding can distort your organisation!

It is important to ensure that the need for funding and income generation although part of the strategic process does not dominate or distort it. Here are ten ways in which the wrong kind of funding can distort your organisation's strategy and even damage the organisation.

1 **It's all short termism.** Year-to-year funding scrambles make long-term planning hard. The organisation lacks security and finds it hard to recruit and retain staff. A lot of work goes into starting projects and activities, but an absence of any long-term funding means that they never really deliver their potential.

2 **Capital rich – revenue poor.** Going for a capital project such as a new building can create a major focus for fundraising effort. Often in the enthusiasm to raise the capital amount the annual running costs are underestimated or overlooked.

3 **No-one pays for the centre.** Many funding bodies are keen to fund projects and specific programmes rather than simply grant aid an organisation. This can create an organisational imbalance – new work is developed, but the organisation's infrastructure and management systems are not sufficient to support and service them.

4 **Cash flow kills.** It is not just how much you get from a funder but it is also when you get it. Having to chase money and dealing with uneven patterns of income and expenditure (such as spending most of the money in the first half of the year, but not being paid until the third quarter) can test an organisation's management and financial capacity.

5 **Strings attached.** Sometimes funders will attach restrictions as to how a fund can be spent or earmark it for a particular purpose. A problem occurs if meeting such directions distorts the work of the organisation. Workers at a youth development agency noted that their work was being directed to work with 18–24 year olds as that group was seen as a priority to funders. Other groups that the agency considered a priority were being ignored.

6 **They won't last for ever.** Most capital purchases (buildings, equipment, vehicles) will need either replacing with new ones or at the very least repairing and upgrading. They usually depreciate in value.

7 **Fast growth.** Growth can be hard to manage. Rapid expansion of an organisation's services and activities needs to be matched with a growth in the organisation's management capacity and ability.

8 **Uneven growth.** Sometimes one aspect of an organisation's work becomes attractive to funders. Money starts to pour into it. It radiates success and prestige. It is tempting to focus all energy and effort into it. This can cause problems for other parts of the organisation. Care is needed to ensure that long-term work is not lost because a particular area of work has become 'flavour of the month'.

9 **High management costs.** Some forms of funding have high transaction costs. Funders expect regular monitoring reports, performance measures, audit returns and other management tasks. The cost and time of such tasks needs to be recognised and budgeted for.

10 **Didn't want to be here.** Often funding can take you down a path to somewhere that you did not want to go to. Over a three-year period a community regeneration project noticed its work changing from community development to running vocational training courses. The project leader commented 'a pot of money became available to open up access routes back to college – we applied for it and were successful. Although some good work has been done, it has shifted our focus, changed our culture and our relationship to our users – we never wanted to be a mini college.'

Managing funding successfully

Operate short term – think long term

The limitations and frustrations of short-term funding can make longer-term strategic thinking feel impossible. However, to avoid crisis management it is important to develop a longer term view, both of financial issues and of the longer-term strategic development of the organisation. A good business planning process should take the longer view and help the organisation prepare a series of contingencies and possible longer-term plans.

Use the business plan

The business plan can be used as a valuable tool to explain the financial basis of the organisation, alert people to key risks, show that the organisation is thinking strategically and also to make the case for a sound organisational infrastructure.

Influence funders

Involving funders in the planning process can help them to understand the financial realities of the organisation and to see how their possible investment can best be made. Do not be led by funding alone.

As organisations grow there is a tendency to hive off fundraising and create a separate fundraising function. Often fundraisers can see opportunities for future funding or feel that they would be more successful if the organisation developed in a particular way. This can lead to compartmental thinking or even conflict between fundraisers and other staff. It is important that fundraisers are involved in the whole planning process and not simply given a target to meet at the end of the process. They need to understand the whole picture. Equally the organisation needs to decide what it wants to do and then look for funding.

'Soft' strategy missing

A theatre had invested considerable time and money in producing a business plan. External consultants, residential weekends and considerable extra work by the finance officer had produced a final document. The plan looked impressive with detailed objectives, cash-flow projections and measurable business targets.

Three months after the plan's production the theatre's director announced her intention to resign and live abroad. The announcement did not surprise anyone as for the past year she had often talked about her plans. The director had set the theatre up and in many respects it was an extension of her personality. Much of the theatre's 'know how' was carried in her head. She had a considerable personal network of funders, contacts and supporters. Trustees and staff expressed fear and panic about the difficulty of replacing her and how much would be lost when she left.

The organisation had spent nearly a whole year planning. All the *hard* elements (costing, marketing plans, staffing levels) had been properly dealt with, but one of the few things that could have been anticipated had been ignored.

Examples of *soft* strategy could include people, styles of work, goodwill, cooperation and partnerships.

What elements of *soft* strategy need to be thought about in your planning process?

- Mgt team setting
- Mng dhmm nttng.

EXERCISE 17

Identifying the assumptions behind the plan

Think about the implied assumptions behind your organisation's future strategy and plan.

Possible assumptions might include:

- Levels of support – *'The local NHS will want to continue to purchase our services at the same level.'*

- Business assumptions – *'We will remain the main local agency working on this issue.'*

- Levels of need – *'Levels of demand will remain roughly the same.'*

- Internal issues – *'We will probably be able to recruit and keep the same number of voluntary workers.'*

In column 1 describe the assumption, in column 2 note anything which challenges it, in column 3 assess how safe an assumption is and in column 4 note any action or implications.

	1 What is the assumption?	2 Challenges to it?	3 How safe an assumption is it? 1 (not at all) to 4 (sound).	4 Action needed or implications
1.	Maintain level of volunteers	· Recruitment · Turnover · Training	3	· assess special age gap etc · Training plan
2.	Demand will be the same.	· Change in need - contract e.g. debt	3	
3.	Core funding will continue	· Performance · Mentoring service · Monitoring	3	· Set up monitoring system
4.	3 months reserves	· ah - cost	3	· budget control

EXERCISE
18

How clear is the direction?

This exercise is useful to attempt after the main strategic aims of the organisation have been agreed.
If the answers are uncertain or vague then it may mean that the direction agreed is not decisive enough.

If the strategic aims are successfully implemented...

What will be different about the organisation?

Will it be:

- ☐ Bigger or smaller?
- ☐ Doing more things or fewer things?
- ☐ The same users or different ones?
- ☐ Generalist or targeted?
- ☐ Working in the same ways or different ways?

What will be the key differences if this strategy is implemented?

Outreach working

Try to describe the significant changes of the new direction as if you were writing a newspaper headline.

CAB reaches out to the communities

What will still be the same?

Core services will be maintained

What will the organisation do more and less of:

More of:	Less of:
· *Outreach working*	
· *Project work*	
· *partnership working*	

When did you last have a new idea?

Many voluntary organisations pride themselves on being innovative. They see themselves as being dynamic and challenging. What is the reality?

Here is how one worker in a national organisation described her organisation's approach to new ideas.

'If someone has an idea that they want to push for they have to be prepared to run an obstacle course of working groups, consultation meetings and discussion papers. It will take months. Any plan that emerges (and quite a few don't) will have had any inventive or creative element drained out of it.'

Managing new ideas and creating innovation tests many organisations. The following exercise aims to help you to evaluate the capacity of your organisation to be innovative and ensure that the plan does have a creative element.

List any new or dynamic ideas or initiatives that have got off the drawing board in your organisation in the past two years.

What are the factors that encouraged innovation in the organisation?

What are the factors that discourage innovation in the organisation?

What does the organisation do to encourage new ideas?
(possible examples could include having a research and development budget, evaluating current services, encouraging project teams etc).

How could this be improved?

What happens when new ideas or innovative projects go wrong?

What is the balance of the plan between ongoing work and new work in the plan?

How can new ideas, creative strategies and innovative work be encouraged in the planning process?

EXERCISE 20

Scenario planning

Several organisations, notably the military and the oil industry, have used imaginary scenarios as both a learning and planning tool. A possible future situation is described and participants work out how the organisation could respond to it and then evaluate the likely impact of their actions.

A housing organisation developed its annual staff residential day around three scenarios:

1 The decision by a major funder to withdraw its financial commitment by phasing it out over two years.

2 A change in the political control and the managerial style within a local authority. The new leadership would be interested in partnerships and transferring the management of several projects from the public to the independent sectors.

3 A decline in demand. A combination of reasons have led to a sharp fall in the numbers of referrals to a usually busy project. Financial, marketing and service plans need to be implemented quickly.

Staff worked in teams to suggest short-term and long-term action plans, explore options, spot dangers and test out the organisation's current processes.

Extensive discussion followed on how the scenarios could have been anticipated or avoided, the importance of a coordinated response throughout the organisation and the need for contingency plans.

The outcome of the day was that all staff had some experience of strategic thinking, and several outline contingency plans were produced (for example blueprints for possible projects should the opportunity arise).

Three months after the exercise, a similar situation to one of the scenarios did arise which tested the effectiveness of the plans and the process!

What scenarios could you design for your organisation?

> • Funding drying up
> • Change in Management
> • Partnership working increase

What would be your organisation's likely response?

☐ Chaotic? ☐ Strategic? ☐ Coordinated?

☐ Planned? ☐ Delayed? ☐ Bureaucratic?

Strategy planner

Strategic goal *Extend services to the community*

Intended outcomes
- *Improve independence of elderly*
- *Increase awareness of benefits & rights*
- *Improve quality of life*

Key measures
- *No. of clients*
- *Ferward fees*
- *Social interaction - contact with other agencies - referrals*

Activities and outputs needed to obtain the outcomes
- *Assess needs*
- *Work with partners*

Outline work plan	Costings and resources	Review
· *Establish study* · *Partner money* · *board, bmm, GIS*	· *Outreach worker* · *Mgt support* · *Office costs* · *Travel*	

Using the planner

Strategic goal

- Describe the intent.

Intended outcomes

- Describe the intended result.
- How will you measure success?
- What do you want to change or prevent?

Key measures

- How will you measure performance?
- How will you measure results?

Activities and outputs needed to obtain the outcomes

- What work will be needed to meet the outcomes?
- What will be delivered or produced under this goal?

Outline work plan

- Set out the work to be carried out
- Outline costs

Costings and resources

- What are the full costs involved in this activity?
- What staff time is needed?

Review

- What are the key milestones?
- When will progress be reviewed?

Strategy prompt worksheet

This worksheet is intended to encourage staff to identify ideas, options and opportunities for their area of work.

Area of work		
Are the original aims and ideas still valid?	**What has changed in this area since the last plan?**	**What are the likely key expectations and demands?**
Over the next three years what do we think will stay the same?	**Over the next three years what do we think will be different?**	**What are the main trends and developments?**
What is happening in the sector?	**What ideas are there for developing this work?**	**What are the decisions that need taking?**

EXERCISE 22 continued

This is an example of a review sheet compiled by a communications worker in a small national charity. Her main areas of responsibilities are keeping the charity's membership involved and informed, running the charity's information work and lobbying government.

Area of work	Communications work	
Are the original aims and ideas still valid? Yes – strong demand for information.	**What has changed in this area since the last plan?** Much greater use of the internet. Members of the public assume that we run a free public information service. More requests for information and advice from social workers and other professional workers. Increased complexity of enquires – more detailed requests for information.	**What are the likely key expectations and demands** Continued demand.
Over the next three years what do we think will stay the same? Many of our supporters not being online and dependent.	**Over the next three years what do we think will be different?** Likelihood of new legislation – need to encourage supporters to lobby their MP.	**What are the main trends and developments?** Increase in lobbying and parliamentary work. Greater use of the internet. Get little feedback from our members' newsletter. Is it read?
What is happening in the sector? Alliances being formed on policy work. We are seen as the lead agency.	**What ideas are there for developing this work?** Develop an email list and internet based discussion list for our supporters. Can we turn passive members into active supporters, donors and lobbyists?	**Decisions that need taking.** How to organise, support and coordinate lobbying. Should we move towards relying mainly on email and internet communicatio? Should we develop a public information service? Could we charge other agencies (e.g. local authorities) for information and advice work? Are information, communication and lobbying too many functions for one job?

Establishing credibility

A **business plan** needs to make the case for an organisation. It needs to establish confidence in the minds of potential backers that the organisation is competent enough to manage the plan successfully. A manager of a trust that requires business plans as part of its application process commented: 'The idea behind the plan may well be brilliant. But, we need to know that it has the people and systems in place to implement it. We look to the business plan to convince us that the organisation has a track record and that the key personnel involved are experienced in similar activities.'

The business plan can demonstrate this in five ways.

- Show evidence that the organisation has a history of sound practice and good management.
- Establish that the organisation has in place systems and structures that are appropriate to the scale and demands of the plan.
- Show that the organisation has within it a core of personnel with sufficient skills to implement the plan.
- Prove that in the case of new initiatives, sufficient feasibility work on the plans has been carried out.
- Show that it has identified real and potential risks involved in the plan and has taken action to avoid them.

Many voluntary organisations seem reluctant or unwilling to record or market their own expertise, skills and competence positively. The process of collecting this information can have some very useful side effects. It can put them in a much stronger position with funders and purchasers, and it can also increase the organisation's own confidence in itself.

For smaller organisations or newer projects the plan might need to show that there are sufficient support systems around it to help it.

Collecting evidence

The following six points are possible sources of evidence that an organisation has a good track record.

Financial records
Previous accounts and audits could show that the organisation has properly managed its financial affairs in the past.

External evaluations
Recorded evaluation studies could indicate strengths of the organisation.

Feedback from users
Client reaction, client follow up and repeat work could indicate that the organisation is capable of providing a service that people want.

Third party references
Sponsorship from 'eminent' persons could establish credibility. A health group used backing from medical consultants in its business plan to establish credibility with health purchasers.

Client list
A list of current or past organisational clients or partners could indicate credibility particularly if client organisations agreed to act as referees.

Evidence of successful work
Press cuttings, case studies and case follow ups might create a positive feel about the organisation.

Demonstrating organisational competence

A business plan needs to show that the organisation has in place the *systems and processes* necessary to manage the plan properly. The following five areas might provide some evidence.

Good organisational practice

The existence of an equal opportunities policy, complaints procedure, staff development policies and other statements might show that, on paper at least, the organisation is clear about how it should work.

A quality assurance policy

Quality assurance is about three things: finding out from users what is important about how the service operates, establishing minimum quality standards that indicate what can be expected from a service and ensuring that the organisation consistently meets the standards. A quality assurance policy should set out key standards and indicate how they will be monitored and improved. The use of PQASSO developed by the Charities Evaluation Service is one way of showing that the organisation has reviewed itself against standards designed to encourage good organisational practice.

An external award

In some industries the award of the British quality standard, IS9000, is an almost mandatory requirement. Some contracts are only awarded to companies with IS9000 accreditation. All that IS9000 indicates is that the management practices used to manage a system are rigorous and comprehensive enough to satisfy an external audit. It does not comment on the benefit to users of the service being provided or the relevance of the standards set. Another external standard is Investors In People (IPP) which is awarded after an external review of an organisation's staff training and development policies.

Membership of a national organisation

Many smaller organisations or projects could point to their membership of a national organisation as evidence of having back up services such as training, specialist advice and information. The national organisation might also provide some quality assurance function.

Audits and inspections

Evidence of successful external inspections could also be used to show that the organisation is well managed.

Competence of key people

Some business plans include the outline curriculum vitae of all the management team members. This may be going into too much detail, but the following information might help convince backers that the organisation has within it sufficient skilled people.

- Background details and experience of key staff.
- Background details and experience of management committee and trustees.
- Names of external advisers, accountants, solicitors and specialist consultants.
- Relevant qualified staff.
- Staff development policies.

CASE STUDY

Proving credibility

The Family in Crisis charity was a new group set up by parents and some professionals to provide counselling, support and help to families in times of turmoil and stress. Initially the group worked with a network of volunteers coordinated by a worker paid for by a trust. However, changes in community care prompted the committee to approach the Health Authority to discuss how they might work together and the possibilities of financial support.

The first discussion with the Health Authority was positive. The charity's services fitted in extremely well with several elements of the community care plan and with current priorities. The authority asked for a business plan so that they could consider it further.

The draft business plan followed a format set out in a high street bank's new business guide. The section asking them to 'list the relevant experience of key personnel' was initially hard. The Heath Authority officer had commented that it was of concern to them that all 'potential providers were professional'. At first, this was seen by the committee as a weakness as they were 'only volunteers'. Surely the criteria favoured businesses or statutory organisations and put a small voluntary organisation at a disadvantage.

The committee carried out a mapping exercise to list the various skills they had. Amongst the committee's membership were a finance manager in a private company, a retired headteacher, a legal executive and a woman who had set up and now ran a successful small business. The group had within it significant management expertise, but perhaps as important was their combined local knowledge, contacts and personal experience of living with and surviving family crisis.

The charity also had around it a network of people who had during different stages of the charity's history provided help and support. They included two doctors, an assistant director of social services and a psychotherapist. These individuals agreed to form an advisory panel to the charity, separate from the management structure, that would advise the management committee and ensure a quality service.

Despite initial doubts, it was now clear that, for the size of the organisation, the charity had within or around it considerable skills and experience.

Proving that a new project is feasible

Many small businesses (and possibly some voluntary projects) fail because the individuals who start them up are so full of passion for their project that it gets in the way of any genuine feasibility study. The commitment to the vision and dream becomes so important that questions such as will it work and who will pay for it are seen as negative and diversionary. For a new project the business plan needs to set out:

- how the need for it has been identified;
- what the need is;
- what support there is for the project;
- how the proposed project will meet the need;
- what the start up costs will be;
- how the project will researched and tested.

Evidence should be included to show that possible pitfalls and alternatives have been explored. A useful exercise is to try to predict all of the potential questions and challenges there will be to the project and then assemble evidence to answer them. It is also useful in discussing a project's feasibility to identify in the business plan potential risks involved in the project and suggest how that risk can best be managed. It is better to acknowledge a risk first and deal with it than to let someone else identify it as an undisclosed weakness.

A risky business

All organisations encounter some kind of risk. Over the past few years management thinking has encouraged people to be more methodical about risk; to identify possible risks, to assess the chance of the risk happening and to identify action to manage and prevent the risk. The alternative is to avoid risks and try to crisis manage them if and when they happen.

> *"So lets get this clear – you run a hugely over subscribed service to a diverse, demanding and challenging client group delivered by staff employed on a one year contract and supported by volunteers who can walk away whenever they want. You operate in a marketplace and sector that is turbulent and changes fast. At the most your income is agreed for the next twelve months. Yet, you can not see any point in talking about managing risk or future strategy."*
>
> Comments of a new trustee after her first management committee meeting.

In the business planning process it is useful to review the main risks that could threaten the organisation's ability to deliver the plan. The business plan should show that managers have thought through the risks facing the organisation and have in hand a series of plans to prevent them and manage them.

A simple exercise is to identify the key potential risks facing the organisation. Risks can be clustered together into five main groups.

Tangible or physical risk

The more obvious risks – a crisis caused by fire, flood or major event.

Service delivery risks

Risks involved in delivering the service to the user – a duty of care is broken, bad or illegal practice happens or the service is so poor that the organisation could face legal action.

Financial risks

Risk of fraud or of unknown costs.

Organisational risks

Internal factors such as key staff or volunteers leaving.

Political and reputation risk

A threat to the organisation's good name and standing – a local branch gets bad publicity for the organisation as a whole.

Market and business risk

A risk in the organisation's environment – a change in demand or the entry of new forms of competition.

It is important to keep risk in perspective. One manager commented that the risks involved in his organisation were so great that he wondered why anyone stayed around!

A simple risk management framework is useful in discussing risk and identifying long and short-term action.

Each risk is assessed against:

- the likelihood of it happening;
- the impact of it;
- action needed to prevent it;
- contingency plans to manage it.

CASE STUDY

Managing Risk

The Management Board of a community regeneration agency identified six key risks that they needed to manage.

	The likelihood of it happening	The potential impact of it	Action needed to prevent it	Contingency plan
Risk 1: All our funding is short term! Risk that projects all close in 18–24 months time.	Medium. Depends on our ability to secure new funds or extensions to existing funds.	Critical issue.	Start developing exit strategies for each project. Open discussion with funders.	Must develop new projects.
Risk 2: We are dependent on a small team of volunteers – risk that some volunteers might leave.	Medium. Need to recruit new volunteers.	Important that we stay a volunteer agency – we do not want to be reliant on paid staff only.	Increase volunteer recruitment. Develop volunteer retention plan.	Run volunteer recruitment campaign. Develop succession plan.
Risk 3: Cash-flow risk: some of our funders pay late or in arrears – we might not be able to pay our bills.	High. Increasingly being paid late by the local authority.	Threatens our financial security and ability to pay staff.	Set up monthly cash-flow monitoring process. Discuss with council.	Set up loan facility. Renegotiate payment schedule in service agreements.
Risk 4: Poor relationship with local authority – risk that councillors don't like us and could cut our core funding.	Unknown. Hard to know what the council think of us.	Increased concern about our relationship to the council.	Talk to council officers and councillors to establish how they see us. Invite them to visit us – renew relationships.	Find new contacts in the council who will support and champion our work.
Risk 5: Risk that other agencies might move into this area and start winning contracts.	Medium.	Depends if we cooperate or compete.	Identify who might be moving in – is there a possibility of working together?	Develop strategies on how we can work together and not compete. Work out what we do best.
Risk 6: Our building is old, dilapidated and costly to maintain – risk of safety breach or higher maintenance and repair costs.	The building is getting worse! Needs action.	Could be serious. Risk of accident or longer-term risk that building gives off an entirely wrong image.	Do Health and Safety inspection of building. Draw up ideas and plans to improve the building. Set up meeting to discuss our concerns with the landlord.	Depends on response from landlord. If negative consider building move and set up capital fund.

Approaches to risk

Be open about risk – risks are inevitable.

Develop 'early warning systems' for risks – what would indicate that you are moving closer to the risk?

Ensure that each risk is managed – someone in the organisation should be named as being responsible for monitoring each risk, ensuring that preventative action is being taken and that the risk is regularly reviewed and reported on.

Discuss the risk before you get to it – build consideration of risks into all project appraisals and new plans.

Benchmark your risk management – find out and compare how you manage specific risks compared to similar agencies.

Learn from risks – when something goes wrong, consider why. What could you have done differently?

EXERCISE
23

Proving your track record

A business plan should show that the organisation is capable of achieving its plan. It will need to show evidence that the organisation or the key people within it have the competence and experience to manage the plan successfully.

What evidence do you have of the following elements:

Sound financial management

A consistent quality of service.

Effective response to needs.

Good management practice.

What other strengths or organisational assets need highlighting in the plan?

Presenting the business plan

Putting the business plan on paper is an important task. The document needs to be concise, present the plans for the organisation and convince people that the organisation is credible. The plan has to be of use both externally and internally.

A business plan needs to give an honest appraisal of an organisation's development to date. It should note weaknesses and setbacks, as well as strengths and achievements. Some of the most effective plans are the ones that give a full picture of an organisation, and also clearly indicate what action management will be taking to improve performance where it has been lacking.

There is sometimes a problem with releasing a business plan that could be of value to a 'competitor'. The manager of a training centre experienced this problem when required to produce a business plan for a tender to manage a government training programme. She explained that: 'Our business plan contained details of how we cost our work, staffing levels and management arrangements. This information represented the product of years of work of trying to get the service right. We have always worked in a very open way, but I would be unhappy if some of the agencies we now compete with had sight of it. We did submit it, but on the condition that its circulation was restricted.'

The business plan itself followed a format similar to the one set out in this chapter. It was made available to funders and purchasers, who could request any further information. The one-page executive summary was attached to the business plan as a covering document and also used in presentations about the organisation. It was particularly useful for dealing with politicians who had little time to read the full document and only really needed to know the overall direction. The summary document was a freely available publication circulated to the public. The action plan was described by one staff member as a 'management bible' and regularly used by staff working to the plan.

The executive summary is particularly important. It is easy to get lost in the detail of the plan itself. It is important to remember that many potential backers use the summary, or in its absence a two-minute glance through the full document, to get 'a feel of the plan'. This first impression can often greatly influence future considerations. The executive summary should highlight the main features of the organisation, set out its direction and make clear what is expected from others.

Style is important

Careful thought needs to be given to the style and format of the business plan itself. It is useful to list the main messages (no more than five) that you want the plan to convey and organise the rest of the information and evidence around them. Some business plans suffer from being written by people who are so close to the organisation that they cannot see it as an outsider would. Obvious pieces of information are forgotten, jargon is used and assumptions made. It is worthwhile to get someone distant from the organisation to read it through or to edit it.

The tone of the document is important. It needs to convey the message that the organisation has gone through a rigorous process to arrive at it. The language needs to be practical and active. It is not a bland policy statement. A useful exercise is to read through the draft and check that all statements can be backed up and evidenced and also that targets and commitments are clearly included in the detailed plan.

CASE STUDY

A one-page executive summary –
Eastside Business Agency

The Agency is a registered charity and established as a company limited by guarantee. Established in 1987 it operates in the east side of the city, an area of declining employment, high adult unemployment and social deprivation. The Agency's mission is:

'The Agency exists to support a viable and sustainable local economy. To provide high quality advice, training and support to emerging or newly created small businesses. In carrying out this mission it will ensure that highest standards of quality and equal opportunities apply throughout.'

The Agency's seven strong staff team provide initial advice for those considering self employment, practical help with business start-ups, training and consultancy, joint marketing and continued contact with new businesses in their first three years of operation. We deal with an average of forty-five new or potential new businesses at any one time. A recent evaluation shows that the Agency has helped to create 126 new businesses in Eastside employing nearly 300 people. Thirty-nine per cent of our clients are from the Black and Asian communities.

The Agency has developed successful partnerships and funding arrangements with the City Council, the Training and Enterprise Council and the Eastside Regeneration Partnership. One of the high points of last year was the award of the Investors in People standard as a recognition of our commitment to staff development.

This two-year business plan has two central themes. The consolidation of the Agency's work and the development of new services to help established businesses survive the difficult trading climate.

The plan puts forward four strategic aims. The first two will consolidate our existing advice, counselling and information services and continue our popular business training programme. Our third aim is to encourage practical cooperation and joint marketing of existing businesses. Our fourth aim is to pilot new ways of providing assistance to businesses approaching or facing insolvency. This is a new area of work for the Agency and is in response to growing enquiries from our clients.

The plan sets out how this strategy can be achieved with backing at an equivalent level from our current partners, the gradual closure of our grants advisory service and the creation of a new post of marketing support manager.

The organisation is now an established and proven Agency working within the inner city. This plan sets out a two year future for its continued success.

The structure of a business plan

Section	Content	Key messages
An 'executive summary'	Brief outline of mission, values and context. It should highlight the proposed direction, key benefits and make the case for the organisation. A one-page three minute read.	No more than one page. Highlights key messages.
Introduction and mission	The mission statement in full. Explanation of purpose and duration of the plan.	What is the organisation for? What does it stand for? Vision and values? Outcomes?
The organisation's background	A brief history of the organisation. Its legal status and registered office. You need to include basic and factual information to help readers get a picture of your organisation: ■ Status of the organisation: legal status. ■ Relationship to any parent organisation. ■ Scale of operation: where you work, what you do and who with. ■ Size of the operation: number of projects,staff and turnover.	Factual information only.
A summary review	A short review of the organisation to date. Stress strengths, achievements and external recognition to date. Readers may expect to see some honest appraisal of weaknesses. A SWOT analysis is often used to display this information.	Need to show that you have looked objectively at the organisation.
Future trends	An outline of how the organisation sees its future environment developing. Refer to likely needs of users. The plan needs to show that thought has been given to likely external developments.	Show that the organisation is outward looking and has a good understanding of the context.
Strategic direction	What assumptions underpin the chosen direction? What will be the main direction of the organisation's work? What will be its main priorities? What will be different?	Shows that the organisation is focused.
Strategic aims	Statement of aims for the medium term. The specific objectives for each aim could be listed or a brief summary of them given.	Outline plans to guide the delivery of the plan.
Implications	Areas or work that will be dropped or phased out should be noted. Organisational, legal or any other key implications should be listed here.	How will the organisation need to develop or change in order to meet the plan?
Financial implications	How will the plan be funded? Income and expenditure projections for first year and estimates for following years. Listing of financial assumptions behind the plan. Statement of key financial policy (e.g. pricing policy) and evidence of efficient management. (e.g. cash-flow forecast).	That the organisation is taking a strategic approach to funding.
Track record of organisation	Making the case for the organisation. Showing that it has the management competence and experience necessary to manage the plan. The past experience of the organisation and its key personnel could be listed. A list of critical success factors.	It can deliver!
Immediate action plan	Timed action for the first steps in the plan.	The next steps are clear.

EXERCISE
24

Putting the plan together

Make notes about your plan in the spaces provided.

1 Always suggest a solution to a problem.

Acknowledge problems and set backs, but show that you have learnt from them and have a plan. 'Following a review of our unusually high volunteer turnover rates, we have instituted a programme of volunteer support procedures to ensure that all volunteers get an effective and appropriate level of support and supervision.'

> ' Reserves

2 Think about the needs of different readers.

Think about how the plan needs to meet the needs of different readers – staff, volunteers, funders, potential funders… Ensure that it answers the issues that concern them.

3 Use an active language.

The plan needs to feel as if it is a dynamic document that will lead to real work. Avoid a passive language. Say 'we will…' rather than 'it is intended that…' Use short words rather than long ones.

4 Use charts and diagrams to illustrate or emphasise points.

Often readers will simply flip through the plan – a SWOT diagram or a chart showing the balance of intended income might catch their eye and draw them into the document.

5 Watch out for using abbreviations or insider speak.

Check for use of abbreviations or organisational shorthand. 'We have talked to the RDAs about their social exclusion strategy and the latest initiatives from the ODPM.'

Putting the plan together (continued)

6 Use the executive summary.

The executive summary should set out the main points that you want readers to remember from the plan. Write the summary after you have drafted the whole plan. If the executive summary is hard to write it might be because the plan itself is vague and unclear.

7 Highlight the first steps.

If a plan sets out a big and bold direction ensure that the first steps are clear. These first steps should help people to understand what is going to happen.

8 Attach measures.

Suggesting how the plan's strategy will be measured and monitored can add credibility.

9 Edit it as a whole document.

Often different people draft different bits of the plan. The director drafts the strategy, the finance manager does the costings and programme staff write their work plans. This is good and can help to make the plan a team effort. However, it is useful if one person is given responsibility for editing the text to check for consistency of style and that there is flow through the whole document.

10 Ask someone not part of the organisation to be a critical reader.

Ask someone who is not part of the organisation to comment critically on the final draft. Ask them to say what they think the main headline messages are as well as commenting on the document's structure and style.

The elevator test

This exercise, borrowed from commercial venture capitalists, is a simple and challenging way of testing how clear you are about the main messages of your business plan.

Imagine that you are visiting a potential funder at their office to talk over your new business plan. At the reception you press the button to summon the lift. As you wait for the lift you are joined by the chief executive of the funding body. The chief executive has met you before and asks why you are visiting their organisation. You explain that you are dropping off a copy of your new business plan, in the hope that it might lead to funding.

The lift arrives and you both enter it. The chief executive comments that she will not probably have time to read your plan and asks you what the main messages of your business plan are and why they should back it.

It will take 3 to 4 minutes for the lift journey. You are unlikely to get another chance to talk directly to the chief executive. What would you say?

Review

- How easy was it to identify the main messages?
- What are the main messages that you want readers of the plan to remember?
- How well does the plan present them and highlight them?

EXERCISE 26

Evaluating your plan

Make notes about your own plan in the spaces provided.

Does the plan create a clear sense of purpose or mission that all involved in the organisation can work for?

Are all the strategic aims and detailed objectives in the plan consistent with the mission?

Are you confident that you have adequately gathered information about possible external events, trends and possibilities that will affect your organisation's future?

On a continuum ranging from 'bleakly pessimistic' to 'wildly optimistic' evaluate the main decisions and aims within the plan.

Bleakly pessimistic   Wildly optimistic

●━━●

Do any of these decisions and aims cause you concern?

continued

On a continuum ranging from 'wild guess' to 'guaranteed forecast' evaluate the main forecasts and projections in the plan.

Wild guess   Guaranteed forecast

Do any of these forecasts and projections cause you concern?

On a continuum of 'mission impossible' to 'will be easy to achieve' evaluate the specific objectives and work commitments set out in the plan.

Mission impossible   Will be easy to achieve

Do any of these specific objectives and work commitments cause you concern?

Evaluating your plan (continued)

List the five main messages that you would like readers of the plan to retain:

1 ....

....

2 ....

....

3 ....

....

4 ....

....

5 ....

....

How clearly does the plan convey these points?

How will you know if the plan has worked? What feedback and monitoring systems will you use?

What will be the first steps after agreeing the plan? What will be the plan's immediate action plan?

Making it happen

Several organisations invest time in the planning process, produce a business plan and then file it away. It is forgotten until it has to be worked on again. The plan remains a paper document that gathers dust on the shelf. There are three reasons why this might happen.

- The plan never really dealt with the realities of the organisation. It is all about how people would like it to be in a perfect world.
- The process of putting the plan together never engaged the people who needed to implement it. The managers or external consultants who drove the planning process never created a feeling of ownership throughout the organisation.
- The plan itself is fine, but managers do not have either the time or the skill to manage the changes involved.

There are five issues that need to be addressed.

1 How to turn strategic goals into delivery plans.
2 How to monitor the plan's progress.
3 How to identify the management action needed to deliver the plan.
4 Building performance – how trustees and managers can ensure that it happens.
5 When and how to update the plan.

A Board member of a national organisation described performance management in her organisation as follows: 'Ready, Aim – Fire does not really apply to our organisation. We spend a lot of time getting ready – producing policies, doing training, carrying out research, talking about the process. We are forever altering our aim – agreeing strategies and writing plans, but we never get round to firing! A lot of brilliant and exciting plans simply never happen.'

This chapter discusses:

- creating a culture that gets things done;
- turning a strategy into a plan;
- monitoring the progress of a plan;
- managing performance.

Creating a culture that gets things done

In many ways writing the plan is the easy job. Turning it into action, getting people to take responsibility for it and ensuring that action is taken is the real hard work. To do this and to build a working culture that supports and encourages performance, a number of things are needed.

An emphasis on outcomes

In a performance culture the emphasis is on achieving an outcome and less on the detailed methods used to get there. Work should be defined as an intended outcome rather than an activity.

Outcome	Activity
'Establish a self managing and representative user forum.'	Train and support user forum members.
'Increase the numbers of people from low income households attending our events.'	Do outreach work in disadvantaged areas
'Reduce the number of household accidents suffered by elderly people.'	Run an accident prevention publicity campaign.

Outcomes are about achieving a pre-set result. The focus is on the ends and not the means. A wide range of activities and interventions could achieve the outcome of reducing the number of household accidents. Describing the outcome allows some flexibility in how to get to it.

Clarity of expectations

Everyone should know what is expected of him or her and everyone should know what everyone else is expected to do as a result of the plan. The language needs to be clear and unambiguous. A useful way of doing this is to set out how you will know if something has been a success.'

A bias for action

Several management writers have used the term 'a bias for action'. This means building an atmosphere which is about wanting to get things done and being focused on the task. Sometimes, this can be about overcoming procrastination or not doing something until a perfect plan is agreed or everything is in place. Often this involves agreeing to stop discussion and move to action. A less than perfect plan might be better than no action at all.

A crucial element is helping people feel that they have responsibility for implementing an element of the plan. The objective is to make people feel that they 'own' the elements of the plan that they will deliver. This is about creating personal responsibility, ensuring that people are recognised as being responsible and delegating responsibilities for drawing up the detail of the plan as well as delegating responsibilities for making decisions and managing budgets.

A first step is to ensure that once the plan has been agreed responsibility for delivery is then clearly assigned. A useful way of doing this is to go through the plan and identify every task, commitment or intention and then to allocate each one to an individual so that it is clear exactly who has the responsibility for ensuring delivery. Things do not happen unless they are clearly allocated to individuals for implementation.

CASE STUDY

Rolling the plan out

The management team of an environmental organisation spent time changing how they organised the delivery of their new strategic plan. In the past, the implementation was not planned. As one manager commented, "Once the final draft of the plan was agreed by our Board it was as if people assumed that things would happen as if by osmosis."

The organisation adopted a new approach:

'We got staff to write their bit of the plan. For example at a strategic level we agreed to change how we involved and supported our member groups. Once we had agreed what we were doing in the strategy we asked our field workers to write the operational plan setting out how they would implement the strategy. They drafted a work plan with clear targets. Management team then approved their plan. On the whole, it worked; in the past the operational plan would probably have been given to them. Getting people to draft their own plan assigns responsibility – they are more likely to work on it if they have produced it.'

Management decisions: 'We delegated decision-making. We told our resources manager that she was responsible for upgrading our technology,

she had control of the budget and she could appoint and supervise suppliers. She saw it as her bit of the plan. Her line manager's role was to provide support, advice and check on progress, but not to get involved in the detail. In the past she would have had to have spent a lot of time checking with managers before she could spend any money or authorise any action.'

Individual coaching: 'Once the plan was agreed managers met with each member of staff on an individual basis to discuss what the plan would mean for them. These meetings looked at how their role might change, agreed priorities and also identified what training or support individuals might need. One of the main benefits of these meetings was that it helped us to check that people really understood the direction the organisation was going in.'

Appraisal: 'We included a section on the business plan in our six-monthly appraisal meetings. The contribution that an employee had made to implementing the relevant parts of the plan was reviewed. Having it in the appraisal system was a useful reminder both for managers and staff.'

Turning a strategy into a plan

Once agreed, it is important that the implementation of the strategy is planned. A simple technique is to identify the different tasks involved in the strategy and turn them into an action plan.

For example, a health promotion project might decide that one of its key priorities was 'to encourage and support schoolteachers in promoting healthy eating habits.'

The first step is to list all the tasks necessary to implement this priority. A useful way of doing this – sometimes called a 'work breakdown schedule' – is to draw up a list of all the tasks. At this stage the size of the task or the order in which it should be tackled is not important.

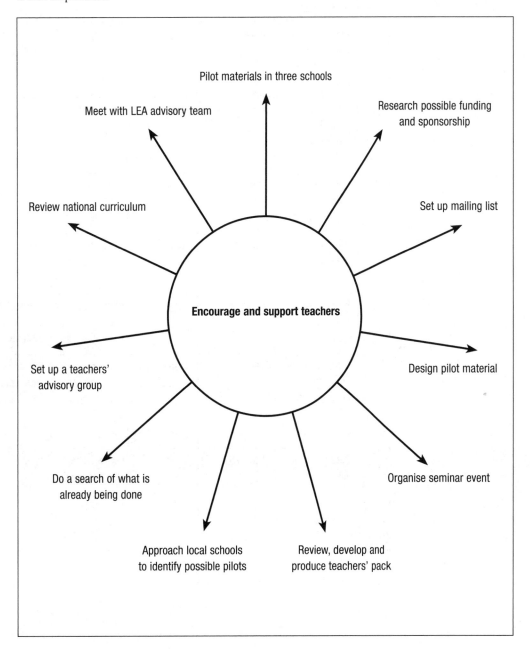

Once all the tasks have been identified the next step is to put them into a logical order – by working out which tasks are dependent on others happening first.

Task order	Task	Start date	Time needed	Resources needed	Responsible	Notes
1	Do a search of what is already being done.	Week 1.	1 day.	Internet.	Sally.	Produce brief for team.
2	Review national curriculum.	Week 1.	1 day.	Internet.	Bob.	Note to team.
3	Meet with LEA advisory team.	Week 2.	Half day.	Time.	Bob and Sally.	Do after 1 and 2.
4	Approach local schools to identify possible pilots.	Week 2.	2 days.	Mailing via LEA. Phone calls.	Bob, Sally and Helen.	Do after 3 – Get LEA to supply contacts.
5	Research possible funding and sponsorship.	Week 1.	1 day.	Use Funder finder.	Helen.	Do file note.
6	Set up a teachers' advisory group.	Week 3.	3 days.	Team to suggest possible people.	Sally.	Plan for first meeting in week 6.
7	Design pilot material.	Week 4.	8 days.	Computer; books; budget of £250.	Bob.	Do after 1.
8	Pilot materials in three schools.	Week 8.	6 days.	Materials. Feedback sheets.	Bob to deliver. Sally to evaluate.	Report to advisory group in week 10.
9	Review, develop and produce teachers' pack.	Week 10.	20 days.	Computer; designer; print; budget of £500.	Bob and Sally with input from pilot teachers.	Drafts ready in week 12. Back from printers in week 14.
10	Set up mailing list.	Week 15.	2 days.	Contact lists from the team mailing database. Pack materials.	Helen.	Mail out pack and invites to launch in week 15.
11	Organise seminar event.	Week 16.	4 days.	Book venue. Do programme mail out. Budget of £700.	Bob and Helen.	Seminar in week 18.

Using a Gnatt chart

A visual way of showing the plan is as a Gnatt chart. An example is shown on page 109.

A Gnatt chart is a simple way of showing what should be happening at a particular time, it highlights potential problems and overload (e.g. too much happening at one time). It also allows for a visible way of monitoring progress and achievements.

A Gnatt chart

	Week 1	Week 2	Week 3	Week 4	Week 5	Week 6	Week 7	Week 8	Week 9	Week 10	Week 11	Week 12	Week 13	Week 14
Research Current provision	■													
Review national curriculum	■													
Meet LEA Advisory team		■												
Find pilot possible schools		■												
Research Funding & sponsors	■													
Set up advisory group			■											
Design pilot material				■										
Pilot material in 3 schools						■	■							
Review & develop pack								■	■	■				
Set up mailing list										■	■			
Organise seminar											■	■	■	■

Monitoring the progress of a plan

A simple way to monitor the implementation of the plan is to use a traffic light system. Progress on every aim, commitment and target is labelled against a traffic light:

RED   No or very little progress has been made
No results
It has stalled

AMBER   Progress in hand
Not complete yet

GREEN   Successfully completed
A result!

CASE STUDY

Monitoring progress

A campaigning organisation used the traffic light system to monitor the implementation of their plan. Here's an excerpt from their report:

	Status	Comments	Action
Set up Scottish office	Red	Staff shortages. Cost of offices greater than predicted.	Director to revise budget. Report on progress and options to Board in June.
Develop network of contacts in each parliamentary constituency	Amber	Contacts in 218 constituencies so far. Taking longer than we expected.	Concentrate on key marginals. Produce lobbying material for contacts to use.
Establish alliance of similar organisations	Amber	First meeting held. Launch event planned for the summer.	Article in newsletter. Review at September Board.
Revamp, redesign and relaunch campaign bulletin	Amber	Redesign completed. Awaiting feedback on the design.	Complete consultation in three weeks.
Identify supporters in parliament	Green	Cross-parliamentary group being formed. Successful Westminster reception held.	Article in newsletter. Director to report on what next.

Once progress on each activity has been judged, action plans can be drawn up;

For the Red items, some analysis might be needed. Why has no progress been made? Is the aim no longer relevant? Have circumstances changed that now make the plan impossible, more difficult or even undesirable. If we are to press on with the Red items what do we need to do differently? Do we need a different implementation plan? Closer supervision, more active support and tighter monitoring might be needed. If we decide to cancel a Red item and not to go ahead with it, then we need to revise the plan and reallocate the resources and time originally budgeted for.

We need to check that the Amber items are on course. Are they where we expected them to be? Is there a danger of things slipping or overrunning? It is worthwhile to check that the next actions are clearly agreed and allocated.

The Green items should be acknowledged, recorded and celebrated. Progress can create more progress. It is useful actively to communicate that progress has been made and that the plan is taking shape.

Managing performance

Often the hardest part of managing is for the manager to know where to exert limited time, energy and effort.

One established technique is to identify those factors that managers need to focus on if they are to be successful. These factors are known as critical success factors. They are the keys to the successful implementation and completion of the business plan. They are the things that the organisation believes it has to get right if it is to meet the plan.

Success factors are usually a mixture of 'hard' elements (things that are tangible and easy to measure such as outputs) and 'softer' issues (such as processes, working culture and styles of work).

It is important to limit the number of factors. Too many will lead to a lack of management focus. Once agreed, managers should work out exactly what it needs to do to work on each issue and draw up clear and measurable action plans for each factor.

One management team attempted to draw up a list of critical success factors for their work. The final statement came from a session in which managers listed the things that they needed to change about how they managed, the things that they needed to improve and, importantly, the things that they needed to keep doing well. The final list was arrived at after some considerable negotiation within the management team. Responsibility for leading particular items was allocated to team members and review dates set. The critical success factors became the agenda for the management team for the coming year.

CASE STUDY

Developing critical success factors

The Halfway project provides practical help and supported accommodation to people with learning difficulties. It employs 38 staff and operates in four local authority areas.

After reconsidering its mission, agreeing a strategic direction and priorities it set about identifying the key elements that it would need to work on to get from its current position to the intended one set out in the business plan.

After identifying specific aims for the organisation (e.g. to develop a new service in a particular location) it also agreed eight critical success factors that managers would need to work on to manage the successful completion of their aims and objectives. It would have been possible to have had a much longer list. However, the team felt that it was better to focus all their effort on the eight points rather than to try to cope with a longer list.

The critical success factors were as follows.

1 Much better communication between the main office and projects. Must feel that we are all part of one organisation. More attention to team work.

2 Need to reduce paperwork and duplication of systems. Enhanced use of new technology.

3 Better financial management system. We need to know exactly what each activity or project costs and have better control of costs in order to negotiate contracts properly.

4 More attention on securing the long-term commitment of our current individual and corporate donors. Persuading existing donors to give regularly and feel a strong loyalty link with us.

5 Our name, image and identity needs reviewing. Need for crisper, more modern and better understood public image.

6 Need to develop our skills and expertise in marketing, negotiating and costing service agreements and contracts.

7 Must develop a commitment to innovation, experimentation and new work. Innovation must be encouraged and rewarded.

8 Need for the two senior managers to spend more time on the strategic development of the organisation and less on detailed 'micro' managing.

The critical factors were reviewed regularly at team meetings and by the Board.

Building performance – how trustees and managers can ensure that the plan happens

Performance management can be described as a four-stage framework.

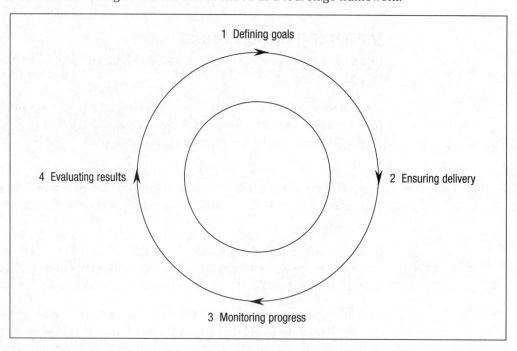

Stage one

The first stage, defining goals for individuals, is about ensuring that people understand what is being delegated to them and what is expected of them. Some things are easier to define then others – for example it is usually easy to define time and money – 'it needs to be ready by the end of the month – don't spend more than £400 on it.' Other factors such as quality ('it must meet user needs') and process issues ('users must feel they were involved') are harder to define. Delegation must be clear and describe the required result. The person carrying out the task must know:

- what exactly they are expected to deliver;
- what resources are available to them;
- what decisions they can make.

Delegation is not just about handing out work, it is also about delegating decisions.

Stage two

In the second stage, it is important that individuals are able to get on with the task. A plan needs to be agreed and resources need to be controlled. However, some flexibility must be allowed. Too much planning can lead to a lack of responsiveness as the plan is implemented regardless of feedback and changing circumstances. Managers will need to help people involved in delivery by coaching, providing guidance and support, but not by taking the work over.

Stage three

The third stage is about having a monitoring process that identifies progress, ensures that things are on track and flags up potential problems. Two issues are important here: first having an early warning system to indicate problems before they become a crisis and second a system that recognises progress and achievements. Forms of monitoring can include the following.

- *Agreeing intended milestones in advance.* Milestones are key points on the road. It is useful to break a bigger plan into a series of milestones and estimate when it is anticipated that the milestone will be met. For example, one of the early milestones in running a fundraising campaign might be to 'have recruited and trained a volunteer campaign team'.

- *Regular supervision systems.* Having regular one to one meetings between the person delivering the work and the supervisor is an effective way of reviewing progress and planning the next stage.
- *Formal systems such as a Gnatt chart.* Formal systems such as a Gnatt chart (see page 109) are an established way of planning and monitoring progress. As the work is done tasks can be marked off on the chart. This is a very quick and visual way of showing that delivery is on track.

Stage four

In the final stage results need to be evaluated. The fact that part of the plan has been completed should be communicated both internally and externally. It also provides an opportunity to give feedback, acknowledge effort and to learn from what did and did not work.

CASE STUDY

After the plan... more planning

The managers of Hillgate Care recognised that their newly agreed business plan would require radical change for the charity. The charity was well established and had provided care and support schemes for a range of adults with learning disabilities. The new plan was based on a recognition that the organisation needed to change, embrace best practice and also follow up opportunities to expand into neighbouring local authorities. The plan had four main strategic priorities.

- To encourage and support the involvement and participation of the service users throughout.
- To broaden the income base by expanding into neighbouring local authorities.
- To develop a community business to create employment for some users.
- To develop a home support service to support some users living independently.

The management team agreed to set up three implementation groups to draw up action plans and lead the work. The three groups were:

1 *A business/service development group:* this group was charged with developing a business case for each new service and for setting up a marketing campaign to develop new business.

2 *A staff development group:* the team recognised that the plan would require new skills in the organisation. This group was given the responsibility of setting up a staff training programme focused on user involvement and also a programme for staff moving from a centre to an outreach role.

3 *An organisation group:* the organisation group was given the responsibility of ensuring that the organisation's infrastructure could cope with growth. The group developed an action plan to look at what new systems and processes would be needed to support expansion.

All the groups were established as fixed-term projects for three months. Members of staff were appointed to each group and were asked to give a minimum of three days and a maximum of six days to work on the group. Each group was asked to prepare an action plan for their work which was approved by the management committee. The action plans were structured around six key issues.

Success criteria: How will we judge success? What is the overall goal?

Key activities: An outline of the programme of work needed.

Work plan: A timed programme of the key tasks, events and activities.

Resource need: A statement of financial, human and other resources needed to accomplish the plan.

Milestones: A plan setting out key review dates.

Responsibility: Named lead responsibility for implementing the plan.

The charity's director commented that she had learnt three things as a result of the process.

1 The importance of moving from strategy to detail. There is a danger that planning gets stuck at the level of mission and overall strategy. The implementation planning is about making it real and agreeing the first steps in getting it moving.

2 The value of involving staff in planning implementation. By involving staff from across the organisation in drawing up the implementation plans we created real communication and encouraged people to feel that they were involved and owned the plan.

3 Things do not happen unless a responsibility is allocated. We went through every line of the plan and made sure that an individual was responsible for ensuring that action happened on every commitment and target. Attaching a name to a plan and ensuring that progress is checked makes it real.

In managing performance three issues often need tackling:

Being prepared to act

It is important that managers act. Often problems or a failure to deliver are ignored in the hope that things will somehow get better. Failure to act can lead to things drifting and small problems becoming a crisis.

Managing failure and set backs

It is inevitable that things will go wrong – deadlines will be missed, budgets will over run and mistakes be made. How failures are dealt with is an interesting test of an organisation's culture. Often failures are either hidden or all the focus is on apportioning blame. In a performance culture the emphasis needs to be on spotting and resolving the issue quickly and learning from it.

Manager's role

In all of this the style and role of mangers is critical. In a performance culture a manager's role is to provide the direction and to coach and support people. It is not their role to do everything or to micro-manage every detail of the implementation of the plan.

Management committees and implementation

Trustees can play a key role in keeping the plan alive. Committee members can bring a level of objectivity and detachment to a project, as they are not (or should not be) directly involved in day-to-day operations. The following ten ideas are all practical ways that a committee can drive the plan.

1 Regularly revisit the plan.

   Make sure that the plan is discussed at committee meetings. It can provide a useful tool to take stock on progress, ensure accountability and identify the need for new strategies.

2 Build strategy into all meetings.

   It is easy for a committee to spend all of its time on day to day reporting and operational matters. Try to ensure that meetings have a strategic dimension to them – reviewing current activities, future thinking and planning.

3 Make sure managers keep to the plan.

   The committee can help managers to deliver the plan by ensuring that they use the plan in their work. The plan should provide a guide for future development and action.

4 Develop some key performance indicators for the plan.

   The process of measurement will often help to ensure implementation. The regular collection, circulation and analysis of performance information will help to identify progress and also act as an early warning system of potential problems and blocks.

5 Set aside review sessions for the plan.

   At least once a year the committee should review the plan to check that the strategy is still relevant and being acted on.

6 Check that the assumptions behind the plan are still valid.

   In any planning process assumptions about the future are made (e.g. 'number of volunteers will remain the same' ... 'referrals will stay at the same rate'). It is useful to record the main assumptions that you make so that you can review them in the life of the plan. If the assumption proves to be incorrect the plan might need rethinking.

7 Focus on the plan's key priorities.

Keep the plan's main priorities firmly on your agenda. Watch out for 'good ideas', urgent opportunities and other factors reducing your focus. The hard part of having priorities is saying what you are not going to do.

8 Highlight success.

When elements of the plan have been successfully completed make a point of letting people know. The process of recording progress and sharing success can increase morale internally and also increase the confidence of external stakeholders such as funders.

9 Circulate the plan to new committee members.

As new people join the committee ensure that they are given the plan and have an opportunity to talk it through. The plan can be a valuable way of learning about the organisation and understanding the work in hand.

10 Don't allow drift.

It is easy for an organisation to drift from issue to issue or be driven by other people's priorities. Make sure that everyone in the organisation understands the strategy and manage carefully the temptation to add things in. If you need to change the strategy do so formally, making it clear what is coming out as well as what is going in.

CASE STUDY

Making sure it happens

An experienced chair of a trustee Board describes her role in making sure that the plan is followed through.

'In two organisations I have worked in there has been a sense of relief when the plan is agreed and signed off. It disappears. It is almost as if people want to "get back to normal". I have adopted three tactics:

The performance of the plan is a major topic at the chief officer's annual appraisal. We go through the plan and look at what they have done to ensure progress. Knowing that this is going to happen does give it some status.

I make a point of seeing the plan as a work in progress. I regularly refer to it in trustee meetings. If an idea for a new project comes up I will ask how it fits into our strategy. As trustees we regularly go back to it.

I pick out two or three commitments in the plan and make a point of asking about them. Two years ago our plan made a commitment to move towards more accessible opening hours. Three months in, it did not look as if this would happen, as it would involve some difficult negotiations with staff. I decided that I would push this issue. I regularly remind our managers of it and ask for progress reports. I try not to get involved in the detail of managing how to do it – that's their job. Despite the difficulties, some improvements have been made. I honestly think that if I had not decided to champion the issue and push for it then it would have fallen away.'

When to update the plan

Sometimes there is tendency to see business plans as being carved in stone – once agreed they cannot be altered over the course of their lives. In reality all plans need to be updated, revised and if necessary changed. Business plans may need revising for the following reasons.

■ New unplanned and unforeseen developments happen in the life of the plan. Something happens that was not foreseen when the plan was being drawn up. A major international disaster might require an immediate response from a relief agency. The disaster might also change future funding projections and intended work plans.

■ The assumptions upon which the plan was built are no longer valid. The thinking behind the plan no longer holds water. For example a surprise election result might change the political direction and priorities of a local authority. So past assumptions about levels of support might need to be rethought.

- Circumstances change. Opportunities do not emerge in line with a planning timetable. New demands, needs and opportunities need to be considered and responded to in the life of the plan.
- The organisation's resources change. Occasionally the resources available to an organisation will change. Fundraising projections may not work out or assumed resources become unavailable. For example a charity with a large investment fund might find its income projections are altered by changes in stock market performance.
- There is a poor or negative response to the plan. Reactions to the plan from key groups such as staff, users or funders might be so negative or unsupportive as to merit a rethink of the organisation's strategy and priorities.

It is much better to change a plan deliberately and clearly than to let things drift or ignore the plan.

The following issues should be followed through in updating or changing a plan.

1 *How big a change?* Is it a temporary blip or a minor issue that does fundamentally change the direction of the plan or is the change such that the existing plan's premise is outdated or no longer credible? A major issue will require a rewrite of the plan. A more minor issue might just require the reordering or reprogramming of the operational plan.

2 *Avoid absorbing change.* A regional manager of a national charity described how despite having a well established planning system local managers were expected to fit in new work and find the time to respond to new demands. This led to overwork, teams and individuals being overstretched and a feeling that the formal planning process lacked credibility as agreed plans were ignored or overwritten. It is better to take stock, review the plan and deliberately agree what needs to change. This process stops crisis management.

Take something out for everything that goes in. Usually a change in the plan involves more work. A useful rule is that for every new task, commitment or piece of work the organisation will have to move resources from somewhere else and therefore reduce resources and time spent on an existing commitment to do something new.

3 *Communicate the change.* It is important to communicate changes in a plan to relevant parties. Staff need to understand how the new plan might affect their work. It is also worthwhile to talk with key funders to ensure that they understand the nature of the change. This may involve having to renegotiate expectations.

Throughout this it is helpful to see business planning as an ongoing and continual process rather than a document.

Index